THE FATES OF
ILLUSTRIOUS MEN

MILESTONES OF THOUGHT

Giovanni Boccaccio

THE FATES OF ILLUSTRIOUS MEN

Translated and abridged by

LOUIS BREWER HALL

Alfred University

FREDERICK UNGAR PUBLISHING CO.

NEW YORK

MILESTONES
OF · THOUGHT
in the History of Ideas

General Editors

HANS KOHN
The City University of New York

SIDNEY HOOK
New York University

All royalties from the sale of this book
have been assigned to the
JOHN FITZGERALD KENNEDY MEMORIAL LIBRARY
Boston, Massachusetts

INTRODUCTION

Boccaccio's *The Fates of Illustrious Men* (*De casibus virorum illustrium*) is a very important document dating from that formative period of Western thought during which the Middle Ages came to an end and the Renaissance began. *The Fates of Illustrious Men* has qualities that are medieval; it has qualities that are of the Renaissance; and it has qualities that are its own, a blend of the two. To separate these qualities and to understand their importance it will be necessary to recall some of the facts of Italian history.

The thirteenth and fourteenth centuries encompassed the period of the great tyrants of Italy. The death of Frederick II of Hohenstaufen left the city-states with no outside coercive force, and every state of any significance—Florence, Milan, Venice, the Papal States, Naples—became interested in expanding its borders. The fight for survival resulted in each state, large or small, putting its fortune into the hands of a dictator, a "Captain of the People." The cunning, severity, and debauchery of these rulers have become proverbial. Entire cities were sacked, their population massacred. Tyrant followed tyrant, and within the cities themselves masses of inhabitants were exiled, their property confiscated. The exile of Dante Alighieri is only the most famous example of many. In Perugia, Pandolfo dei Baglioni, nicknamed the Perugian Satan, killed a member of the rival Raspanti family. In reprisal they killed him, and thirty of his relatives. In Boccaccio's Florence the tyranny of Walter de Brienne, who took the empty title of Duke of Athens from his father, lasted from 1343 to 1348. Boccaccio tells Walter's story in *The Fates of Illustrious*

v

Men, but Walter's malevolence and license were neither unique nor comparatively excessive.

However, this period of inter- and intra-urban warfare was also a period of material growth and prosperity, especially for Florence. Frederick II's death put an end also to the minting of his coinage, and in the void Florence issued her own gold florin, which became the world standard. The economy of Florence was based on the wool trade, but the great chronicler of the early fourteenth century, Giovanni Villani, tells that in 1338 there were eighty banks in the city. The difference between usury and legitimate interest was established and compound interest was discovered at that time by some banker now unknown.

The third decade of the *trecento* was a period of prosperity in Florence, but in the fourth a depression developed. Many of the city's banks, especially those of the houses of Bardi and Peruzzi, had lent heavily to Edward III of England for his wars in France. These wars bankrupted him and his creditors, and, with the defeat at Lucca, Florence suffered from such modern phenomena as runs on its banks and great unemployment. And the forties came to a close with the terrifying plague of 1348, described by Boccaccio at the beginning of the *Decameron.*

It was against the license of rulers and against the general acceptance of material prosperity that Boccaccio directed *The Fates of Illustrious Men.* He intended it as a warning that debauchery, orgy, and cunning would not go forever unpunished, and for this purpose gathered together historical examples of such excesses. He borrowed from Biblical history, starting with the first sinner, Adam, and ended with the history of Italy, but mainly he went to the history of Greece and Rome to find rulers whose misdeeds equaled those of his contem-

poraries, but who unlike them (or so it seemed to Boccaccio) died in misery. Sardanapalus, King of Assyria,
whom Boccaccio blamed for inventing the featherbed,
spent his life in perverted carousal and sloth until the
Medes invaded his kingdom, whereupon he threw himself on a pyre. Appius Claudius' legal machinations to
seduce Virginia brought on her death as well as his own
—a warning to all corrupt judges. Mark Antony, like
Adam, Samson, and Hercules, was a victim of feminine
allure. For *The Fates of Illustrious Men* the Roman
emperors review their crimes, and by means of their
stories Boccaccio demonstrated that the rewards of license had always been the same and had always been
governed by the laws of a single, universal ethic. As
the sins of the Roman rulers resulted in their downfall,
so the sins of the fourteenth-century princes would result in theirs.

In the decade of the fifties Florence was ruled by the
guilds of her merchants and artisans, an experiment with
an oligarchy of the middle class. While Boccaccio expressed opposition to princes, at the same time he by no
means supported any kind of democracy. Rather he supported the aristocratic ideal, the uncorrupted prince.
According to Boccaccio, middle-class persons made bad
rulers and invariably returned to their "natural" level.
These opinions were generally held throughout the
seventeenth century; we can find them expressed in Ed-
mund Spenser's *Fairie Queene*, Sir Philip Sidney's *Arcadia*, and Shakespeare's *Coriolanus*.

Against the second characteristic of the age of tyrants,
its belief in materialism, Boccaccio advocated the ideal
of voluntary poverty. This is a very old ideal, and at
the end of the Middle Ages it seemed to hold a special
appeal all over Europe. In English literature it was expressed by Chaucer's Povre Parsoun who "koude in litel

thyng have suffisaunce," and it also characterized the beliefs of John Wyclif and the Lollards. In *The Fates of Illustrious Men* Boccaccio combined the ideal of poverty with an admiration for rural life. In the chapter "Poverty Applauded," Book I, he said: "How wonderfully beautiful and holy it is to engage in simple tasks with you, oh Poverty; to enjoy the country and solitude, to despise excess, to contemplate things celestial in the shade by silvery streams." The Renaissance was marked economically by a shift from a rural- to an urban-centered economy, and at the same time in literature by a resurgence of the pastoral element that idealized the peace and tranquility of the past age. The pastoral dream that Boccaccio suggested as an antidote to the materialism of the fourteenth century was fictionalized in the sixteenth in Jacobo Sannazaro's *Arcadia*, Luigi Alamanni's *Opere Toscane*, Sidney's *Arcadia*, Lodge's *Rosalynde*, and finally satirized in Shakespeare's *As You Like It*.

While *The Fates of Illustrious Men* re-emphasized the pastoral ideal for the Renaissance, it also took cognizance of a very new idea, the ideal of complete loyalty to the state. To the Middle Ages, giving unquestioned devotion to any political entity was almost unknown—indeed impossible in the complicated network of fealties that encumbered any area large or small. The word "state" as it is used today was just coming into the language, and was probably first recorded by Marsiglio of Padua in his *Defender of the Peace* (finished about 1324), but was popularized in the next century by Machiavelli in *Discourses on the First Ten Books of Livy*. The ruler for whom Boccaccio has the most praise in *The Fates of Illustrious Men* is Marcus Regulus. A prisoner of the Carthaginians during the first Punic War, he was given permission to leave so that he might effect an exchange of prisoners. But at Rome he argued against the exchange. It would accomplish little, he explained, to give back healthy young soldiers for one old man whose usefulness was over. Then Regulus, true to his word, returned to Carthage and death by torture. Regulus, according to Boccaccio, is an example of that rare ruler who not only gave his life for his country but also resisted the temptation of booty and plunder. Boccaccio expressed his indignation with those Florentines who served in the army only for booty, and elsewhere in *The Fates of Illustrious Men* his anger is directed against those who refused to pay taxes (a type of income tax had proved unsuccessful in Florence).

It was Petrarch, Boccaccio, and the other Italian scholars of the *trecento* who gave the name *il medio evo* to the period between the time that Latin became "debased" and the time it was again reborn in the *rinascimento*. The preponderance of classical personages in *The Fates of Illustrious Men* made the work seem very modern to its readers in the fourteenth and fifteenth centuries. Writers during the Middle Ages usually brought their Roman ancestors down to their own level. In *Roman d'Eneas,* an Old French adaptation of the *Aeneid* dating from the beginning of the twelfth century, Carthage is a medieval walled city, albeit with marble walls, and Dido's castle a Byzantine palace with that great medieval luxury, sufficient indoor lighting. Palamon and Arcite in Chaucer's "Knight's Tale" fight a medieval tourney in classical Thebes. In *The Fates of Illustrious Men,* on the contrary, the Romans are no longer thought of as contemporaries. Boccaccio realizes the distance in time between the *trecento* and the days of ancient Rome. Instead of bringing the Romans into Florence, he takes his readers back to the Empire. For his readers in the twentieth century, however, Boccaccio presents a much more brutal picture of classical history than we are used to. His insistence on describing the different methods of execution has, of course, not been influenced by the late eighteenth-century ideas of humanitarianism and sensibility. In this aspect the fourteenth century was much closer in spirit to classical life than we are today.

Still another change is reflected in Boccaccio's attitude toward history. He continues to use history as a guide for virtue, the attitude he inherited from his predecessors; but he also manifests a search for truth for its own sake, the attitude which distinguished historians who came after him. He avoided the popular medieval encyclopedias, like that of Vincent of Beauvais. Whenever he consulted Orosius' fifth-century history of the world, he seems to have carefully checked its statements. Throughout *The Fates of Illustrious Men* Boccaccio frequently uses phrases like "It is reported," "the ancients do not tell us," and "it is generally believed." His last history, "About Philippa of Catania," is especially interesting for in it he tells us who his informants were and what information he received from them.

Vergil was revered by Boccaccio as the greatest poet, of course, but the Florentine recognized the limitations of the *Aeneid* as history. The story of Dido in *The Fates of Illustrious Men* is not Vergil's, but was taken from Justin's epitome of a lost history of Trogus Pompeius. For his sources Boccaccio generally used those Latin handbooks and histories which the *trecento* considered the most reliable sources. Hyginus' *Fables* proved a useful handbook with its long lists, some of which were organized around the manner of death of famous Greeks and Romans. Valerius Maximus' *Memorable Acts and Sayings* and Seutonius' *Lives of the Caesars* provided Boccaccio with ideas and anecdotes. He consulted Josephus' *The Jewish Wars*, the chronicle of Eusebius as translated by St. Jerome; Gregory of Tours' *History of the Franks*, and many other works. But his most important and significant source was Livy's history of Rome, *From the Founding of the City*. Petrarch was instrumental in helping to establish the text, and like Boccaccio found in Livy's narrative a dramatic contrast in moral standards between the Romans and his contemporaries. In a fictional letter addressed to Livy, Petrarch said, "I am filled with a bitter anger against the customs of today when men value nothing but gold and silver and desire nothing but sensual pleasures." Boccaccio depended on Livy for much of *The Fates of Illustrious Men*, and his popularization of Livy and Roman history contributed vitally to the re-evaluation of the classics that was a characteristic of the Renaissance.

The Fates of Illustrious Men is important not only for its contribution to the rebirth of the classics, but also for its contribution to the history of the drama. It provided a transition between medieval drama and that of the sixteenth century. The mysteries, miracles, and *laudi* all concern themselves with some aspect of the story of mankind—from the fall of Adam, through Christ's redemption of man on the cross, to the Last Judgment. The miracles, of course, were concerned with one of the saints' lives. The very nature of these stories is such that the ultimate resolution had to be in Heaven. This fact underlies all great literature of the Middle Ages, whether the work be *The Divine Comedy* of Dante or Chaucer's *Troilus and Cressida*. In *The Fates of Illustrious Men*, however, the characters are punished here on earth, and this change in setting from Hell to Earth is one of the milestones of literary history. *The Fates* was directly imitated in England in the *Mirror for Magistrates,* for example, and this work, in turn, influenced Shakespeare in his treatment of such characters as Richard II, Richard III, and Macbeth.

Boccaccio finished *The Fates of Illustrious Men* about 1358. He was probably midway in his forties (his birthdate, 1313, is not altogether certain) and was surely working on the collection less than ten years after he had finished the *Decameron.* There is no evidence to support the idea that he suffered a decline in powers in his Latin works, nor that he suffered an acute religious melancholy as is sometimes suggested. The same narrative techniques are apparent in both the *Decameron* and *The Fates of Illustrious Men,* although in the later work his narrative technique is more highly synthesized. Sometimes complete chapters in his sources are reduced to a few sentences, and pages of Livy are reduced to a single paragraph. But in both the *Decameron* and *The Fates* we find descriptions which achieve great effect with few words, as in the account of Sardanapalus or the characterization of Vitellius. The destruction of Troy gives a sense of chaotic doom with electrifying speed. In both works there are lively exchanges of conversation —as between Poverty and Fortune, Boccaccio and Brunhildis, or between Tiberius, Caligula, and Messalina. In *The Fates of Illustrious Men* Boccaccio does not relate events alone, but also portrays the effect of these events on the characters involved—for example, the effect on Theseus of the death of his son, on Xerxes of the defeat of his armies, the effect (or lack of it), on Nero of the murder of his mother, the effect on Brunhildis of her approaching death.

In comparing the *Decameron* and *The Fates of Illustrious Men,* it must be realized, however, that the *trecento* would have found a qualitative difference between the works that today is no longer so pertinent.

The *Decameron* was a work in Italian about ordinary
people in a familiar setting. Because of its language and
subject matter it lacked the serious importance of *The
Fates*, an importance produced by the historical weight
of its characters and expressed in its language and style.

Even within the limits imposed by this seriousness,
Boccaccio still transformed the manner in which history
and biography had been written in the great collections
before his time. *The Fates of Illustrious Men* is the
only collection that makes use of the vision technique
to organize the continuity of the stories. As Boccaccio
sits in his study, a cavalcade of all the great names of
history pass as before him. Many of them still bear
the physical signs of their earthly end. Dido is pale
and her face covered with tears; Sardanapalus' robes
are still scorched; Appius Claudius is ashamed of his
passion, and tries to pass by unnoticed. This use of a
vision framework enables Boccaccio to keep the general
order of historical time, yet still permits him to enliven
the presentation with continual motion and variety. The
framework also allowed him to present two or more of
the personages involved in a single historical event. We
have the stories of both Priam and Agamemnon, of
Gaius Marius, Pompey, and Anthony. It is a fundamental
ideas of *The Fates of Illustrious Men* that all rulers,
conqueror and conquered, meet the same end, and the
vision framework made this novel point of view seem
natural. Earlier biographical collections of illustrious
personages, like Petrarch's, St. Jerome's, or Isadore of
Seville's, did not use this method; nor had Boccaccio,
himself, in his first collection, *Concerning Famous
Women*. By the time of the fourteenth century the
use of a vision of this kind is little more than a literary
device; but to Boccaccio's contemporaries it would appear less artificial than to us. To them, what does not

fall within sensible experience is not necessarily less true. A vision is actually closer to the ultimate reality of a neo-Platonic Heaven than sensible experience is, for only in a vision can this ultimate reality be "seen."

At the time when he was working on *The Fates of Illustrious Men* Boccaccio was also ambassador of the Florentine republic to the Papal court at Avignon, was gathering material for his life of Dante, and was engaged in the study of Greek with an extraordinary though repulsive character, Lorenzo Pilato. Petrarch called this man with his long, unkempt hair and beard a "great beast." Both Petrarch and Boccaccio tolerated him while he was translating the *Iliad* and the *Odyssey* for them, but neither of them learned any appreciable amount of Greek from him.

The evidence that Boccaccio in his last years was not inhibited by a severe religious melancholia has been greatly strengthened by the recent discoveries of Professor Marvin B. Becker of the University of Rochester. In the state archives of Florence he discovered that Boccaccio had been arrested for playing zara, a dice game, on July 23, 1367. Professor Becker commented, "If this were in fact Giovanni Boccaccio, then it would mean that his last years were not always spent in pious anxiety." *

The Fates of Illustrious Men became immediately popular and contributed far more to Boccaccio's repu-

---

* *Renaissance News* XVI (1963), 298. The entry states that "Iohannes Bocchaccii" from the St. Peter Major section of the city was seized for the playing of zara by the retainers of the Lord Captain of the People and released on the payment of seven lire ten soldi. Dr. Sergio Camerani, Director of the State Archives discounted the evidence as referring to another "Bocchaccii," not only because of the spelling but also because Giovanni Boccaccio lived, at least six years before, in the Quarter of St. Felicity. Professor Becker has meanwhile confirmed the spelling as referring to the author.

tation for two hundred years than did the *Decameron*.
In 1395, only ten years after Boccaccio's death, a cardinal
of Spain said that *The Fates of Illustrious Men* was full
of many excellent examples and fine admonitions not
inferior to those of Valerius Maximus. Boccaccio was
quoted as one of the authorities for *The Vindication of
the Duke of Burgundy*. During the evening of November
23, 1407, the Duke of Orleans, brother of the King of
France, was killed in ambush. The Duke of Burgundy
admitted full responsibility, and this document was
drafted in his defense. Boccaccio was cited with other
authorities such as Aristotle, Cicero, Seneca, Thomas
Aquinas, St. Augustine, and John of Salisbury. In a play
presented thirty years after this, Boccaccio is one of the
dramatis personae with Terence, Horace, and Juvenal.
The drama is a religious mystery, *The Revenge of Our
Lord Jesus Christ*. Boccaccio appears to tell the story
of Augustus Caesar; then Horace recommends that he
tell the story of Nero. During the period immediately
after Boccaccio's death the *Decameron* was little known.
Petrarch discovered a copy only accidentally toward
the end of his own life. At the beginning of the fourteenth century Duke Humphrey had a French translation made for his library, but the tales were not generally
in circulation until the middle of the sixteenth century.

For this translation of *The Fates of Illustrious Men*
the Paris edition of Jean Gourmont and Jean Petit (1520)
has been utilized, because it is a good representation of
Boccaccio's first edition and because it is now generally
available in a facsimile edition. In a few places the
Gourmont-Petit edition has been corrected on the basis
of its apparent source, Manuscript Latin 6069L of the
Bibliothèque Nationale, Paris. About half of the original
tales and links have been selected for *The Fates of
Illustrious Men*, based on their representative character

as well as for their importance to the history of European
literature and of ideas. No attempt has been made to
reproduce Boccaccio Latin style in English. Boccaccio
was one of the humanists influential for the revival of
Renaissance Latin; but to achieve the same effect on
the modern reader that his style probably had on the
trecento reader it would have been necessary to imitate,
for example, Milton's style in the *Areopagitica*. A com-
promise has resulted in a style that is simpler, yet clear
and accurate, it is hoped. Many thanks are due to the
British Museum, London, and to the Bibliothèque Nationale for allowing their printed editions and manu-
scripts to be freely consulted.

Louis B. Hall

SELECTED BIBLIOGRAPHY

BOCCACCIO, Giovanni. *De casibus virorum illustrium,* ed. Gourmont and Petit, Paris, 1520 (Gainesville, Fla., Scholars Facsimiles and Reprints, 1962).

BRANCA, Vittore. *Boccaccio Medievale* (Florence: Sansoni, 1956).

CAMPBELL, Lily B., ed. *The Mirror for Magistrates* (Cambridge: Cambridge University Press, 1938).

FARNHAM, Willard. *The Medieval Heritage of Elizabethan Tragedy* (Oxford: Blackwell, 1956).

HORTIS, Attilio. *Studi sulle Opere Latine del Boccaccio* (Trieste: J. Dase, 1879).

HUTTON, Edward. *Giovanni Boccaccio, a Biographical Study* (London: John Lane, 1910).

LIVY, Titus. *Ab Urbe Condita,* Loeb Classical Library (Cambridge, Mass.: Harvard University Press, 1935-47), 14 vols.

PATCH, Howard R. *The Goddess Fortuna in Medieval Literature* (Cambridge, Mass.: Harvard University Press, 1927).

SCHEVILL, Ferdinand. *History of Florence,* rev. ed. (New York: Frederick Ungar Publishing Co., 1961).

CONTENTS

The First Book

The Second Book

The Third Book

The Fourth Book

The Fifth Book

The Ninth Book

INTRODUCTION

*What the author hopes to accomplish
for the reader with his stories.*

I was wondering how the labor of my studies could benefit the state when I recalled the conduct of illustrious
princes. These rulers are so attracted to vice and debauchery, are so unrestrained, that it is as if they had
put Fortune perpetually to sleep either with drugs or
with spells; then with iron bands they clamp their little
empires to an adamantine foundation. I realize how they
not only oppress others with their power but also, which
is worse, with foolish temerity rise up against the Worker
of all good Himself. I was astounded. I condemned
their folly and admired the everlasting patience of our
Father.

Then I found what I had been looking for. What
would be more charitable to them in their license, more
useful for their eternal salvation, than to call them back
to the straight road if possible? Up to the present time
many writers, well known for their excellence and piety,
have often labored diligently on this problem. I believe
it is my duty, though my skills are not equal to theirs,
to try to penetrate their guard, then to shatter an illusion
that may cause their death.

To be sure, people who make a habit of sensuality are
usually difficult to influence and are never swayed by
the eloquence of history. Therefore, I shall relate examples of what God or (speaking their own language)
Fortune can teach them about those she raises up. And,
so that there can be no accusation against any specific

time or sex, my idea has been to present succinctly—
yet still with useful detail—those rulers and other famous persons, women as well as men, who have been
overthrown from the beginning of the world until now.

Some famous people will be missing from my histories,
for who could live long enough to finish the infinite
labors required to include them all? Therefore, from
among the mighty I shall select the most famous, so
when our princes see these rulers, old and spent, pros-
trated by the judgment of God, they will recognize
God's power, the shiftiness of Fortune, and their own
insecurity. They will learn the bounds of their merry-
making, and by the misfortunes of others, they can take
counsel for their own profit.

In order that an unbroken succession of stories be
not tiresome to the reader, I think it will be both more
pleasant and useful from time to time to add induce-
ments to virtue and dissuasions from vice. For a lofty
beginning and success in this work, I humbly pray to
Him who has all power, that He favor and watch over
what I write so it may add glory to His name.

ABOUT ADAM AND EVE

*Human fate and fortune
had its beginning in the Garden of Eden.*

In my mind I ran over the lamentable catastrophes of
our ancestors, so that from among the multitude of those
who have been cast aside I could choose the patriarch
of the unblest. Suddenly two people presented themselves, so old they seemed scarcely able to move about.
The man began to speak:

"By the will of God, we, the first man and wife, have

filled Heaven, but by the persuasion of the devil, we tested the instability of Fortune. And so no one else has more right to stand at the beginning of your work."

I stared at these decrepit souls, wondering about them. They were born not according to nature, but were the parents of all, and before their downfall were the inhabitants of Paradise. Amazed, I began, and I willingly chose them before all others.

Adam was of the soil of the earth, formed by the finger of God, given life by the breath of God; and made a man whole and mature from a field which afterward was called Damascene. After he gave names to the other animals he was taken into the Paradise of delights. When he took his first rest, the Highest of Fathers skillfully created Eve from his side, mature in body, not for infliction (as people are married today) but joined to him for true solace. Possessors of a place so celebrated and so exalted, they were restrained by one law only, that they please one another joyfully. They began to go around observing everything, contemplating the delicacies of the abode and enjoying them. They saw flowers unnumbered, all with a thousand colors, living in perpetual bloom. Trees stretched to the sky with pleasant shade formed by their eternal leaves. Among these trees stood the famous Tree of Life and the remarkable Tree of the Knowledge of Good and Evil. In addition, from a spring, very pure and lively, rivers flowed in a full stream, wonderfully bubbling with silver waves, a certain sweet jingling and easy flow irrigating all the earth. The woods, uninspected by human eye, stirred with a soft breeze, the chattering sound of the birds went unheard.

What more could there be? There the sun was larger, the moon more silvery, the stars brighter, and the serenity undisturbed. Nothing was harmful, all was complete security and eternal tranquillity. To the first inhabitants of this very desirable land God was a companion in place of the clattering crowd; and, truly, because of this Presence all things were joyful. A shining band of angels, who by nature knew the desires of all creatures, fulfilled the duties of servants, everywhere helping our great ancestors. Instead of wearing clothes decorated with gems and gold, they kept their bodies nude, a true and never failing splendour. But, so I do not expound on their infinite comforts any longer, let me say the joy of our parents was sublime, even incomparable. But wait a moment. As exalted as all this was, so their lives suddenly fell into almost extreme misery. For while these new inhabitants had, as on the earth, lived free of care, joyous and pleasant, the enemy, moved by envy, was there; and with a false argument, intent on over-coming the laws that were imposed on them, seduced the mind of the woman, and she the mind of the man.

Oh, the blind desire of temporal things! These per-sons, to whom God's gift was the rule of all creation, thought that through disobedience they could make themselves equal to God, and so they began to exist as lowly mortals. This detestable crime was the root of all evil and the downfall of humanity. By this means the doors opened wide, and sin entered victorious into this world. Naked poverty, anxious care, pallid disease, and sorrowing old age are laid to its heavy charge. Slavery, exile, interminable labor as well, and (if I may gather all miseries into one) the instability of fortune; and with all these, the certain death of men, that reduced everything almost to naught. Sinning, they actually condemned all their descendants with them. By their guilt they extinguished the light which had covered them, and when they perceived their shame they sought a place to hide. After they were first reproved, they were driven from their splendorous homeland onto a barren earth, and they reached a land sown with thorns. Spurred by hunger, they sought nourishment by the sweat of their brow. They endured the sky now with its cold, now its heat; they suffered with disease; frequently they heard the roar of thunder and saw the flash of lightning, felt the drive of the winds, endured the wild beasts, serpents, and the fury of the birds, everywhere a thousand perils. They began to fear the death that they had acquired. From this source came mourning, tears, lamentations, repentance, a vain desire for peace, and longing for the abode of happiness and the tranquility that they had lost.

I wonder what they thought when they realized that one of their sons had treacherously killed the other who became a carcass without a soul, a body without motion that was sprinkled with blood, wasted and insensible. Can I imagine what anguish, what horrors, what fears till then unknown were theirs? Then was the survivor a fugitive banished, a wanderer, and finally in the wilderness, hiding in the lairs of beasts, he was pierced by the arrow of his grandchild. We must believe they suffered a newer fate, so much harder and more bitter for them to tolerate. They realized that time covered their hair with gray, and dulled the strength of their bodies with pain and old age. They believed that they were created for immortality, but now found death because of their own crime. When they were exhausted with their great effort, they both saw the earth flower nine hundred times plus thirty; growing old with it and leaving a great army of sons and grandsons in Hebron as descendants, Adam was taken down to Hell and there was his sepulcher. And in the same way Eve died, exhausted by old age.

TIME CONSUMES ALL THINGS

Rather fitly the renowned ancient poets, when they related the fable that Saturn devoured his own children, under the surface of this rough covering, wished to indicate that everything produced in time, represented by Saturn, was doubtless consumed by it. If fire can consume any living thing on the earth, the sword destroy it, water drown it, the earth swallow it up, then time, slipping past, lays waste everything. In a mystic silence, insensibly, while it flows, life ebbs, and what once existed, goes back into nothing as if it had never been. How many emperors once famous, how many illustrious philosophers, how many worthy poets, how many others who in their time earned praise through supreme effort, not to mention others, how many are there whose names have been consumed by time, so that among us there is no memory of them at all? I believe these forgotten ones are without number; and among them almost all before this time in history have vanished, it is not unreasonable to think. The discerning reader, therefore, will little wonder that here in the beginning persons overthrown by Fortune are rather rare. It was long between Adam and Nemrod, the builder of the tower of Babel; and during this interval the ancient writers have remembered almost nothing that at present is regarded very highly. It was a long time between Nemrod and Cadmus, of whose history we are about to speak.

ABOUT CADMUS, KING OF THEBES

*A great king lost his grandchildren in a series
of unlucky accidents.*

Among the ancients it was well known how Europa,
daughter of Agenor, King of Tyre, was raped by Jupiter
in Crete. Because of this misfortune Agenor was angry
and ordered his son Cadmus to search for her, adding
a warning that Cadmus not return to his homeland without her. When Cadmus, together with some companions
he had selected, got aboard his ship, he thought that
to follow the path of a woman was beneath him, and
he went into voluntary exile. Seeking a new home for
himself and his companions, he guided the ship to
Greece, fulfilling a prophecy made by the oracle of
Apollo at Delphi that he would follow a bull, and for
this reason he later named the province Boeotia. After
he had put down a disturbance among the inhabitants
as well as the opposition of the Spartans, he built a city
which he called Thebes, and on the spot was named
king.

His exile seemed happy to him, not only because of
the kingdom, but also because of his brilliant knowledge.
He gave the rough and unlearned people an alphabet
and schooling. To have descendants of his own he took
Hermione as his wife, a woman well known for her
nobility and beauty. She gave him four daughters,
Semele, Autonoë, Ino, and Agave, whose grace and
beauty were spectacular, and Cadmus gave them in
marriage to outstanding young men, who brought him
grandchildren. So the royal youth saw himself a king in
exile (though we know nought of the attractiveness of

the country) and saw a growing city, that he himself had founded, flourishing in joyous prosperity. But among the greatest gifts of Fortune he counted especially his wife and their offspring.

But this was not the end of the story. Semele, pregnant by the love of Jupiter, perished, as is told, when she was hit by lightning, and this event left the kingdom stained by a disgraceful adultery and death. Then Acteon, a superior young man, the son of Autonoë, his daughter, and Aristaeus, in a wood was torn limb from limb by his own dogs, almost before Cadmus' own eyes. In addition Cadmus learned that Agave, at the orgy of Bacchus, a rite celebrated by Theban women, had been aroused against her son Penteus, whom she conceived from her husband Echion. Penteus had laughed at the ritual, and she became enraged and felled him miserably either with a club or a spear. In truth these calamities were scarcely to be endured by a man already fated to unhappiness. But Cadmus was to be made more unhappy from other sources, and he preserved his life, not according to his own will but perhaps according to the plan of God.

Athamas, honored among the Thebans with the title of king, became insane, and he thought his wife Ino was a lioness and his children lion cubs. With a horrible cry he attacked his wife, tore his son, Learchus, from his mother's arms, and with all his strength dashed him against a rock. The grief-stricken mother feared for her own life and fled while Athanas pursued the other children. With Melicertes, she threw herself into the sea from the steep precipice of a mountain, and both perished, swallowed up in the waves. Cadmus, now an old man, thus experienced his greatest tragedy in the deaths of his children and grandchildren, by whose aid he had thought to sustain his last years and carry his name in all its glory to posterity. For a long time he needed peace rather than action to endure his exile, but Amphion, who afterward took over the kingdom of Thebes, drove Hermione and Cadmus, now weighed down with extreme old age, from the country. Mourning, he sought a hiding place among the Illyricans where, almost unknown, he was taken by death. And thus the man who had left the Phoenicians famous and with the Boeotians lived splendorous on the royal throne, died among the Illyricans, twice exiled and obscure.

A GATHERING OF UNHAPPY SOULS

*Cretans, Greeks, and Israelites crowd around
all trying to tell their stories.*

By now the human race, multiplied by many generations, filled the area of almost all the earth, and Fortune demonstrated her rule over all perishable things by her many circumvolutions and by the misery of great numbers of people. Because of the rarity of those who were overthrown before, I was forced to let centuries slip by between one example and another, but now I saw an army of mourners milling around me. Although I sought only one, suddenly there was an enormous number. One stood out from all the rest: Aeëtes, King of Colchis. Because the magnificence and splendour of his riches had never been seen before, the barbarians thought him to be offspring of the sun. With a querulous voice he lamented the arrival of Jason, the Thessalonian, into Colchis; for, by Jason's perfidy, his son Aegialeus died miserably, the golden fleece was seized, Medea fell into

insane lust and fled, and in his old age Aeëtes himself was cast from his glorious height into horrifying
darkness.

Near Aeëtes was Minos, well known for his numerous
titles and accomplishments. Above everything else his
birth was lustrous; he was born of Asterius, King of
Crete, and Europa, daughter of Agenor. Because he was
outstandingly just and was by tradition the one who
brought law to Crete, he was always thought to be the
son of Jupiter. Above all he was brilliant as a king with
throne and crown, but his was also the most famous
marriage of his time—to Pasiphaë, daughter of the sun,
who bore him (indeed he was fortunate) many well
known children: Androgeus, Ariadna, and Phaedra. But
the mournful death of Androgeus, unworthily killed by
the Athenians and the Megarans, was the cause of unexpected unhappiness. However, the unhappiness in his
disturbed soul became the spark of a memorable victory.
After he had declared war, he conquered the Athenians
and the Megarans, and by the guile of his daughter
also killed Nilus, King of Megaris, and both states he
made pay tribute to him. He ordered that each year
they send him youths of noble birth. In public games
instead of a prize he sacrificed them, as solace for the
death of Androgeus.

Oh, how unstable is mortal fame, for surely because
of you, Fame, weeping Minos complained that a cloud
was raised which covered everything with its darkness.
When he discovered the adultery of his beloved wife,
he left, and because of the strength of victorious Theseus,
Athens was released from its yoke. His daughters fled
with the victor, and following Daedalus, he met his
death among the Sicilians at the hands of the daughters
of Crotalus.

Sisara was also present, complaining that when he

had been the prefect to the king of the Canaanites, his huge army was put to flight by Deloora and Barac. He was very frightened of the Israelites, and he stopped his flight when he met Jahel, a wife of the Cinites. After she gave him some milk, for some time he fell into a very deep sleep, and she killed him shamefully with a single blow of a club. But I was procrastinating for too long a time, for I met Jocasta, Queen of Thebes, the most unhappy of all this gathering. She seemed the empress of evil, and were I to work with all my ability, I would not be able to relate all of it.

ABOUT JOCASTA, QUEEN OF THEBES

Jocasta lost her child, but she was avenged in a strange and sorrowful way.

It was really enough for us to enter Thebes once, but the great misfortune of Jocasta made it necessary to return there again. Born into a well known family, she was joined in marriage to Laius, King of Thebes, in the budding of her youth. Joyfully she saw that they had conceived a child. When she was heavy with the child, Laius consulted the oracle of Apollo and learned that he would be killed at its hand. Immediately it was born he commanded it be thrown to the wild beasts. How very painfully Jocasta took this when she knew she had given birth to a boy, I let mothers consider.

The child was given to Phorbas, a royal shepherd, so that he could be left to wild beasts, but found the pity in the shepherd that he had not found in his father. Phorbas had compassion on the age of the innocent child, and arbitrarily changed the royal order. He pierced the little one's feet with a sword, suspended

him from a tree by a reed and left the child crying,
almost on the point of dying from hunger. But immediately another shepherd, a stranger, arrived and cut the
bonds on the feet, which were now swollen, and because
of this the child was afterward called Oedipus. The
astonished shepherd took the child in his arms, and
cursed the cruelty of the person who hung the child
there. A short time afterward the boy was given to a
Corinthian and then immediately and in secret taken to
Merope, wife of Polybus, King of Corinth, who had no
children of their own. They received the child and kept
him while they could, as if the child had been sent
to them by the gods in place of a son.

Oh, how unexpected are the outcomes of events. This
child who was taken from his own mother in the greatest
despair, was accepted by a strange woman in the
greatest joy; the child who was rejected by his father
and condemned to death, was adopted by a complete
stranger as heir to his kingdom. The child who was left
in a forest to die, was taken into a palace to live; he
who was hung naked from a tree, was wrapped in a
royal swaddling and borne in royal arms. The child who
filled the woods with his pitiful cries, now was consoled
soothingly and royally; and he whose feet were speared
by a shepherd, was healed by a king.

But now what happened? Oedipus developed into a
strong and handsome youth, royally instructed in spirit
and manner, but when he learned that he was not the
son of Polybus but had been found in a forest, he was
stirred by a desire to know his father. With deep anguish
Polybus let him go, and after he came into Cirrha he
learned from the oracle that he would find his father
again in Phocis and would finally marry his mother. He
was astounded by this reply, but came into Phocis. A

conflict had arisen between the citizens and foreigners, and Laius made the greatest effort to calm those who were taking up arms. Oedipus allied himself with the foreigners, Laius with the others; and when they met, Oedipus struck Laius with his sword and killed him, not knowing him at all.

Then he went on to Thebes, not recognized as the slayer of Laius. Because of his fame as slayer of the Sphinx, as some are pleased to say, as the son of King Polybus, as other relate, he married Jocasta, still mourning the death of Laius. He was afraid lest he marry Merope, whom he imagined was his mother, and accepted willingly. So what he thought in caution he would avoid, in ignorance he achieved. Indeed, he ruled happily and by his own mother had four children. Jocasta erased both her son and her former husband from her mind, reigning and indulging herself in luxury. She thought she was happy now to have such a husband and such children.

But a terrible plague arose in the city. According to their practice, they inquired what was the cause and what the manner of expiation. Tiresias, a prophetess, told them that the plague would not stop unless the man who killed his father and married his mother was put from the kingdom. And by divine revelation this was shown to be Oedipus. Jocasta could hardly believe this until a certain old-time Corinthian, whom she had called to the kingdom when Polybus died, made it clear to her what had happened. This news blasted their happiness, and filled them with misery. Jocasta bewailed their shameful marriage, and Oedipus wished to die. After he put aside all insignia of kingship, with his own hands he put out his eyes and imprisoned himself in perpetual darkness. His great sadness was further embittered when his children laughed at his blindness, and for most of the rest of his life he harassed the gods with prayers for their ruin.

The gods showed themselves sympathetic to these prayers, and it happened that the desire to rule entered both sons at the same time. Disagreeing, they developed a very sharp hatred which they finally sought to alleviate with this solution: while one reigned for a single year, the other at the same time would remain in exile. But this arrangement rather increased their fury, for Eteocles did not cede the kingdom to Polynices, who sought it after a year had passed. Nor was Oedipus disappointed in his wish for their downfall, because Adrastus, King of the Argives and father-in-law of Polynices, marched against Thebes leading a part of the Greek army. Each side fought many devastating battles, and there are many, perhaps, who believe that Oedipus in his cave heard the varied din of war: the cry of the trumpets, the whinny of the horses, the uproar of the soldiers and civilians, the shrieks of the women; all the manifold turbulence and tumult invaded Oedipus' dark world. He was happy to have obtained an answer to his prayers. It is not easy for me to believe, however, that there are any hurts that can terminate a father's love for his children, and we must imagine that he heard only with the greatest bitterness of heart about the deaths of his sons from the wounds each inflicted on the other, and that in his heart he regretted and bemoaned enormously his past prayers that the gods now had granted him.

Oh, how foolish we are! We bear children but condemn them unjustly. When they are beset by misery, we cannot hate them. Jocasta recalled that she had thrown her child aside, regretted deeply Laius had been killed. She recalled having taken her own child as a husband, who had then left the kingdom and put out his eyes. She still loved her other children, regardless of what they were; one a king besieged, the other besieging and exiled. Finally the land was ruined far and wide, the kingdom laid waste, the sons rushed at each other, swords were wielded in hate, and each succumbed to the wounds inflicted by the other. No longer able to bear such unhappiness, such despair, such dejection, she took the sword with which Oedipus, holding it in his lamentable hands, had killed Laius, and she threw herself on its sharp edge. Both her life and her sadness left her by the wound, and with her own blood she brought a hapless end to her calamities. The wondrous blossom of Jocasta's youth flowered into dry fodder, and the splendor of royal glory turned into smoke and vanished into the air.

So her happiness that had no strong foundation turned to certain tears and led the anxious woman to be the subject of this story. Oedipus, after he lost his father, his kingdom, his eyes, his sons, and at one and the same time his wife and mother, as consolation in his old age was put into chains and driven disgraced into exile by the order of Creon. When or how his spirit, shaken by its difficulties, escaped, I do not remember reading.

THE QUARREL OF
THYESTES AND ATREUS

*An adulterous brother argued with a depraved one
as to who was most wronged.*

I had taken up my pen and thought that I would tell
King Theseus' story, when Thyestes, one of the unfortunate Pelopians, came up to me, exclaiming:

"Please stop, I beg you! Do not write any more. Am
I not more worthy to be remembered than either Oedipus
or Jocasta? If you are so anxious to give one more example of evil and unfortunate people to the future, why
do you leave me behind?"

I stopped, and he continued, "Atreus is a traitor and
rancorous, and is well known to the whole world for
his crimes. I thought he was my brother when he was
really my enemy. What terrible grievances I have against
him for what he did! Ignoring the bright years of my
youth, I come to afflictions that are undreamed of till
now. With great deceit Atreus called me back into the
country from my troubled and unjust exile, just as if he
had forgiven my past wrongdoing and wished me as a
brother to share the kingdom with him. I came back into
the city to the great joy of the Mycenians, but, unaware
of the situation, I fell into the trap. Oh, the false embraces, the treacherous kisses, the tears of joy, the
words of affection with which he received me on my
return. Happy (for he had obtained the prey he sought),
he said that he wished sacrifice to the gods of the country. Not knowing what victims he had consecrated, I
willingly agreed to what he was about to do. In my

naïveté I had forgotten myself and my family because I believed that his heart was as true as he feigned in his appearance. After he had put me at my ease, this monster went to the impious altar with some inhuman companions who knew of the crime. There, in a most secret cave of the house, and not by the hand of a subordinate—his frenzy made him too distrustful, and who was ever more impious than he?—he stabbed my three innocent sons, and from their open wounds streamed their blood and their life. How cruel a rite to the infernal gods in Thrace, let alone to the household gods in Sparta!

"Nor was this enough. As if he were about to prepare a banquet for his distinguished brother, he cut up the delicate bodies of the little boys and placed them on the table as a dish in front of the banqueting father. I do not want you to put your faith only in my words as to whether that was something unspeakable. The sun, observer of all things, is a witness; revolted by so terrible a crime it was hidden by a dark cloud, and then setting its horses going again, went back into its orbit and brought night, which it had driven from the world, back to the Greeks.

"But this was not the end of the horrors. He commanded placed before the thirsty father a cup, jeweled and golden, prepared with a drink, the foaming blood of the innocent children. Unknowingly, I ate the flesh of my flesh and drank their blood. Still, I did not know what had happened until I called my children to me, and the nefarious villain put their lifeless countenances in front of me.

"Granted my exile; granted its punishments and almost unbearable joylessness. And in addition granted the tears, the calamities and the disasters. These I endured in solitary misery. Do you think that anyone else is worthily called more wretched than I, or more cruel than my brother?"

Thyestes had just ended his story when from across the way came Atreus, his appearance proud and excited. He exclaimed:

"What celebrated accuser is this? What horrible old man is this who blames his depravity on others? I am the wretched one; this man is the villain, and I will now tell you everything he did.

"If you were not aware of it, I married a desirable woman, young and beautiful. Her modesty and integrity this embellisher of bestiality corrupted with promises and with sweet talk. He violated my marriage bed, and had children of my wife. I was simple and suspected nothing about my brother. I thought the children were mine. Perhaps you are astonished? Continuously seething with passion, he did not respect the virginity of his own daughter Pelopia, knowing full well what he did, and wanted to do it. From her, it is clear, was born a son, Aegyptus, who ruined the whole family of Tantalus.

"Now you should be horrified, if possible, about the mistake of Oedipus' unhappy mother. But more about that is superfluous. When the kingdom of Mycena, large enough for two, was divided between those two sons, each tried deceitfully to get it all from the other, and from this developed the cause of just exile. I could cleanse myself of these unprecedented and intolerable villainies. Perhaps my strength was not sufficient against his skills, which this faker of miseries himself taught like a master and which he demonstrated by his performance. I judged my misfortune to be extended enough. I did those things for which he himself gave cause. I gave him the children to eat, I confess. But he would have first given them to me, if he had not believed they were his own.

"In short, I suffer from my wife's adultery; I suffer from my brother's deceit; I suffer from the desire for revenge—a common infirmity of mankind. I suffer because I had to be cruel against my own nephews or stepsons. I wished to think that the vengeance balanced the offense. He violated my bed. I violated his table. He conceived his children in a womb that belonged to me. I thought to bury them in his own stomach. In no other way could I return these atrocities to their original state. He wished to occupy the kingdom fraudulently. Fraudulently I threw him into prison and chains —he to whom exile was not sufficient freedom. By deceit, deceit was deceived. Because of these things, I believe I am the most unhappy of men, but he is more savage than all the beasts."

Old Thyestes was excited and leaped forward to reply, but I was disgusted to hear things so bestial and inhuman. I repulsed him and took up my pen to tell the story of Theseus.

ABOUT THESEUS, KING OF ATHENS

The King inadvertently caused the death of his son and set in motion a series of tragic events.

The city of Athens was once the light of Greece, for it was the celebrated nurse of philosophers, poets, and orators. It also had very famous kings; and Theseus, the son of Aegeus, a member of a family which included many of the most renowned, was fated to be perhaps the greatest of them all. He developed into a strong youth, and gave such promise of leadership to the citizens of Athens, long exhausted by war, that they quickly foresaw what he proved to be. The fuzz of his beard was hardly visible on his cheeks when, with surprising strength, he killed the bull which had been terrorizing the countryside at Marathon. Until that time the flower of Attican youth had been wasted in human sacrifices in trying to appease Jupiter.

One of the Argonauts, Theseus returned with Jason bearing glory as well as spoils. With Hercules he went to the Amazons, and, driving back their forces, he defeated them in a fierce battle. He returned in triumph and brought with him Hippolyta, their Queen. Nor during the wedding of his friend, Pirithous, was he honored less because of the danger that came to him from the Centaurs. Noted for their arrogance, the Centaurs had been excited with the wine and the feasting, and they tried to steal Pirithous' bride from him. Theseus' victory over the Minotaur is also worth everlasting praise. He thereby freed the Athenians from paying tribute to the Cretans, and brought back into the city those who had been troubled by a variety of misfortunes and had been driven out. With extraordinary courage he held back the Thebans, and after he had slaughtered many of them, he killed Creon, overbearing because of his new power. Creon had refused the rites of burial to the leaders of the Greeks because his son Mnestheus had been killed in the battle; and by this bloody defeat, Theseus brought an end to these practices.

Who can relate fully his great accomplishments, which added so much to his splendid reputation and to that of Attica? If Theseus did nothing else than gather together those who had been dispersed from Athens, he would have established the greatest reputation among the most worthy and outstanding personages of history; for by this act he gave glory to Greece and the eternal light of philosophy to the world.

Thus honored, Theseus assumed his ancestral throne.

Although it was scarcely noticed, Fortune had arranged the method of his downfall; for a little later Theseus, angry, ordered the death of Queen Hippolyta of whom he had had a son, Hippolytus. Now Pirithous' wife had died of natural causes, and, emboldened by their successes, Theseus and Pirithous mutually swore they would marry only the daughters of Jupiter.

When Theseus returned victorious from Crete and had left Ariadne drunk and asleep on the isle of Naxos, he married Phaedra, whom he originally brought back for his son, Hippolytus.

Pirithous, however, wished to remain true to his pledge to marry a daughter of Jupiter. He asked Theseus to go with him to the depths of the sea and help him bring back Proserpine, daughter of Jupiter and Ceres and the wife of Orcus, King of Molossia. This adventure ended badly. Pirithous was killed by Cerberus, Orcus' ferocious dog. Much weakened by this misfortune Theseus himself was captured, which cast not a little shame on his reputation. What was more dishonorable, however, was that he proved unable to return to the upper world under his own power but needed the aid of Hercules, luckily returning from his victory in Spain. Hercules conquered the three-headed Cerberus and set Theseus free.

Again Theseus returned to Athens to live quietly if chance would have it, but he discovered that the court and the city were disturbed over a saddening state of affairs. Phaedra was inflamed by the handsomeness and charm of Hippolytus, and offered her body to him without shame. He was chaste by nature and refused her, but she became very angry, and when Hippolytus had gone away, she broadcast it about that he had tried to seduce her by force. On his return Theseus believed his wife's accusation without question, and, enraged, ordered his son be found and seized for punishment. Hippolytus was terrified, for he could remember Theseus' former rage against Hippolyta, and he fled in a chariot at full gallop. But while guiding the excited horses on the road with his whip, he came upon some sea lions basking along the shore; disturbed by the clatter, they jumped up and leaped impetuously into the waves again. This so frightened the horses that, even with Hippolytus trying to hold them back, they left the road and ran across a steep, rocky slope. Finally they broke the reins and fell headlong over the incline. The young driver was thrown from the chariot, which overturned and smashed, and it was his ill luck to be caught in one of the reins— I don't know which—and he was dragged at terrifying speed through the thorny underbrush and rocks. He not only was killed, but his body was torn limb from limb on the rubble and spines, and it is impossible to relate just what was left of it. It was indeed a horrifying and doleful sight even to his enemies, let alone his father, to see his body so scattered in the wilds.

Theseus, saddened by the loss of his friend Pirithous, grieved because of his own imprisonment, miserable because of the ugly death of his son, was struck yet another blow. The beloved memory of Hippolytus and his misfortune kindled the fires of love that had been half asleep in the unhappy Phaedra. When she learned and saw Hippolytus' miserable lot, she was repentant too late for the crime she had perpetrated. In tears, she foolishly reevaled her sins to Theseus, already beside himself with grief and mourning. She had scarcely finished when she stabbed herself with the sword that Hippolytus had left when he fled, and her cruel death purged the evil that her passionate attachment had begun.

Theseus turned aside in horror. Moved by paternal

affection he mourned the fate and death of his son, who had been condemned by his own sentence, and he lamented the innocent one bitterly. He was deeply affected and cursed his own heedless credulousness. The blood of his beloved wife, though rightfully shed, filled his thoughts. The joy in his victory over the Centaurs and the liberation of Athens was equal to his misery in the funerals of his innocent son and culpable wife. But graver events were still to take place. While he was enveloped in unhappiness, the ungrateful Athenians rose up against him and drove him into permanent exile— this leader who had called them back into their own country, who had given them their form of government!

What good did his royal lineage do him? What good the glory acquired by his valor? What good his strength? And what did his kingdom avail against hard-hearted Fortune? Everything falls to her impetus, and if anything at all is left to a man flung into misery—but Fortune usually takes everything—then the memory evoked by what is left rather increases the grief than adds to the joy. As we end the tale of his hardships, Theseus is mournful and aged, without honor and joy, spending his last days on one of the smaller Cyprian isles.

A WARNING
AGAINST CREDULOUSNESS

The armed assassin is less difficult to resist than lies and flattery.

It little befits a person to flutter like a leaf in every breeze. It is even more ruinous, however, when those who are endowed with power can put their every wish into effect. Of course, obstinancy often leads to harm, but just as often credulousness leads to destruction. What is more foolish than to open your ears wide to every tittle-tattle as if it were the absolute truth?

Do you think all opinions make equal sense? Certainly nothing is more foolish than a credulous mind. The prudent man refuses no one's ideas, weighs each according to its worth, then deliberates carefully so that he does not make a mistake by a too precipitous conclusion concerning something he does not know anything about. He is like a mental watchtower observing with discrimination who is speaking, and judging what the speaker has to gain; he wants to know who speaks against whom, what actually took place, where and when. He takes anger or calm into account, and whether the speaker is friend or enemy, honorable or infamous.

Theseus, who was otherwise a prudent man, should have determined what were the habits and general nature of his son, and because of his great experience with Phaedra or with his mother, he should have recognized the nature of women. He saw that his son obviously enjoyed the woods, the fields, and the mountains, that he enjoyed trapping birds, tracking wild animals, and hunting with the bow and arrow. He was content to remain a bachelor. He disdained and avoided all women and retreated from marriage, making his home under the sky. The accusation against him was contrary to his true nature.

On the other hand, women by nature are unrestrained, inconstant, untruthful, and continually burn with unsatisfied passion. Although Theseus may have realized there were some chaste women, he could not hold that opinion of Cretan women remembering Pasiphae and Ariadne. And if he, therefore, had a bad opinion of those who deserved it, without thinking he also had a bad opinion of those who did not deserve it. What is more unreasonable than to believe a crafty person is simple, a parricide is harmless, a flatterer tells the truth, a lecher keeps his virtue? It is difficult for anyone to accomplish anything in which he has not had any experience or which he undertakes for the purpose of deception. This is the reason a worker is able to use his tools—a man is known according to his inner nature.

Often I remember laughing when I saw princes walking in public surrounded by a retinue of servants. The doors of their houses had guards who examined everyone for arms. At meals they had food-tasters in case they might swallow anything poisonous. On the other hand they kept their ears wide open and their minds receptive to anyone who was speaking, as if words could not influence, deceive, or poison them. Oh, how foolish was their ingenuousness! We have never heard of a village, no matter how small, the inhabitants of which were all killed by poison, nor any group of people, regardless of its size, who could not prevent an equal misfortune with a little care. Countless tragedies known in every hamlet proclaim that it was the honeyed phrase, the deceptive tongue believed too easily which brought about the downfall of the credulous, the ruin of cities, the destruction of whole regions and their inhabitants, and the subversion of kingdoms. This kind of polished speech does not bring truth to the credulous, but in an instant it excites them, sways them, delights them, accuses them, soothes them, and irritates them. At the same time that it gives them hope, it makes them despair; and like the winds of the sea that blow now east now north, so the clever phrase drives the poor soul now one way and now another.

Nobody puts a guard on his ears or hires a taster for words. Those who have investigated natural phenomena say that there is a species of snake that, when it is sleeping, by a natural instinct recognizes the danger of its being killed by the pipes of a snake charmer. It plugs up one of its ears and deafens the other with its tail. The unfortunate human being, while endowed with more intelligence than any other animal, does not take such care of himself. What am I saying—does not take care of himself? On the contrary, man *wants* to have flatterers around him and seeks them out. He goes out to meet those who conspire in the death of his reason by flattery.

Credulousness is the mother of errors, the stepmother of artifice, the cause of hatred, a precipice to fall over, and always the neighbor of repentance. If we are human, if we examine ourselves, if we are careful, we will follow the authority of ancient laws which abhorred ready credulousness. The laws prescribed that nothing be believed rashly, nothing accomplished precipitously; and that, whenever possible, both sides be heard before a final judgment. While we disapprove of Theseus, we should guard against suffering his misfortune.

A GATHERING OF THE MOURNFUL

Hercules, Orpheus, and others plead in vain to be heard.

I had finished my discourse on the credulous and had turned to investigating other unfortunates when a large group of mourners appeared unexpectedly. Leading them was Althea, Queen of Calydon. She was in mourning attire, weeping copious tears, her hair was snarled, and her face sadly torn by her fingernails. Toxeus and Plexippus, her brothers, had been killed by her son, Maleager, who died after a sacred brand, which was guarding him, had been consumed by fire. Because of this tragedy Althea died.

In this group, too, was Hercules, horribly burned, his beard blackened and tangled, his hair shaggy. He was dressed in the skin of the Nemean lion, carrying a cudgel in his right hand, and his clamor resounded on all sides. He said that for the good of others, with his own strength, he carried out the commandments of King Eurystheus. He was only conquered by one beast, lust, incited in the person of Iole. By her order he arranged and perfumed his hair. He wore rich robes and covered his fingers with jewelry, and to please her he spun thread among the servant girls. How very shameful is an effeminate man! With these degradations he destroyed the reputation he had gained with his earlier deeds. I would have turned my pen to his story, if I did not think it unfitting in my writing that I should also spoil his reputation, which all the greatest poets had tried to extol to the stars and beyond.

After him then came Narcissus, Byblis, and Myrrha, deploring the fires of lust and the great ignominy of their deaths. Orpheus was there too, complaining about the loss of his Eurydice, the unyielding judgments of the other world, and the atrocity of the Bacchanalian women. Marphesia and Orithria, most unhappy, were wailing, contrasting their defeat by the Greeks with their earlier famous victories. Who can give all the names of those approaching? It was a long column, and they all wailed at the same time, so that I could not understand what they were saying. However, King Priam and Hecuba, the most unhappy of all those approaching, solved my problem. I looked through their eyes to their souls, and because they were examples to all the world of the overturn of Fortune, I thought they could not be omitted.

ABOUT PRIAM AND HECUBA

The destruction of Troy seen through the eyes of Priam and his Queen.

Priam was very famous first of all because of his ancestors, for he was descended from Tuscus Dardanus, who, ancient authorities said, was the son of Jupiter and Electra. Aided by a famous start, he was further helped by Fortune. While he was still a boy his city was sacked and his father put to flight, but he was taken away by Hercules, later rescued by his fellow-countrymen and reestablished in his ancestral kingdom. The city was built up again and its power reinstituted. The Trojans collected the wealth of almost all Asia. In addition to all these glories Priam received as wife, Hecuba, daughter of Cisseus, King of Thrace; she was more beautiful and modest than any other woman of her time. Nothing which might add to his enjoyment was kept from this wealthy king. His wife gave him nineteen children of both sexes, among whom Hector was the most famous for his valor, not to mention Troilus and Deiphobus. Other women gave Priam thirty-one children, among whom several were well known and worthy. He had many famous daughters-in-law and was able to see his grandchildren. His kingdom was abundant in wealth and population, and tranquil in a joyful peace. He received more than he desired.

Yet the higher a man rises, the closer he is to mortal peril. This truth Fortune demonstrated in Priam and his family by their wretched end. While the illustrious Priam thought he had all Asia at his feet and measured his happiness by his successes, an idea secretly worked its way into his haughty mind. He recalled Hesione, whom flimsy Fortune previously had erased from his memory. It seemed to him that it would not detract from his felicity if he could wipe out the shame brought about by Hesione's capture. How a little spark driven by a moderate wind can breed a great fire! Although Priam was protected by good fortune, he did not give this heed; and while he thought he was about to extinguish a small spark, actually he stirred up a great conflagration. So truth is proved by trial.

Emissaries were sent to obtain Hesione's release from Telamon, into whose hands she had fallen. But Telamon refused to give her up, having gotten her as legal spoils of war. This angered Priam and he sent Paris with a fleet. He was afraid that Paris was the firebrand of which Hecuba had dreamed when she was pregnant with him. Paris feigned peace and went through the motions of negotiation with the Lacedemonians. Menelaus, however, was away, and Paris aroused the passions of Helen with his good looks and by the story of his adventures. Paris seized her and took her off to Troy, where Priam received him as if he had accomplished his vengeance. This was not only their last happiness, but was also the first bloom of evil and the seed of irreparable catastrophe.

Priam neglected to return Helen, and he saw that all the Greeks with fire and sword had gathered against him on the shore of Rhoeteum. Far and wide around the capital they pillaged and destroyed everything. And for no little time; for ten years Priam could watch the Greeks continue laying waste his entire kingdom. While he observed all this, he was subjected to the most violent attacks. I will only touch on the deaths of the kings who came to help him, and the downfall of their peoples. From the tower of proud Ilium Priam, a stricken old

man, could observe Achilles kill Hector, in whose
strength lay the hope for the safety of the kingdom and
the prosecution of the war. What Priam's tear-filled eyes
could not see was Hector's body disgraced and covered
with dust, tied to the chariot of the victor and dragged
around the city walls through all the dirt and rotting
corpses. It was left twelve days as a prey for dogs. Who
will deny that this terrible end eclipsed his previous
brightness by an eternal cloud? But in this death there
are still other lessons. As a young man Priam was used
to accepting the tribute of kings; but as an old man he
was forced to go into the camp of his enemy, and,
offering the most valuable gifts, beg his son's body from
those who had killed him.

I am silent about Hecuba, whose tears were apparent
enough. For Priam a second loss followed the first. By
the same enemy, by the same hand, Troilus—another
hope of his desolate father—was slain; and though he
had not been the equal of Hector, still Priam lamented
his death with bitter tears. After these deaths, with
great mourning he buried Paris, bloody and cold like
the others, but not killed by the same hand. And then—
so I do not tell the story haphazardly—Priam saw the
Palladium taken, and he realized that all hope of peace
and safety was lost. During the night the Greeks entered
Ilium by a trick and Priam heard the crackling of the
burning houses and the hostile tumult that filled all the
city. From the palace tower Priam was able to observe
the great clamor, the weeping, and the slaughter of the
people, for the Greek soldiers spared neither sex nor
age. The brilliance of the flames routed the black of the
night. Nor was it probably concealed from him that
Andromeda and Cassandra were dragged by their hair
to become slaves of the victors.

The enemy forces completed their victory when they

smashed the bolts and tore the doors off the royal palace. Priam had fled to the family shrines, and saw his son Polites fleeing, anxiously seeking the help of the old man. Pyrrhus followed him and killed him with his sword. Priam, himself feeble, tried in vain to help Polites and was covered with the blood of his fallen son. Then he was pierced with the same sword, and by his death he defiled the altars where once he had made sacrifices. Here he fell, and, because of the fatal wound, his soul, once proud, now tired by age and misery, departed.

In the flower of her youth Hecuba had received honors, distinctions, and glory as much for her family as for her rank. Now an old woman, alone with Priam, she suffered all the dismal unhappiness and the sharp blows of a cruel Fortune. Although she was very wretched after suffering so many reversals, if she had died beside the man with whom she had lived, she would have avoided many more misfortunes. She died finally, not as much because of the span of her years as because of her continual unhappiness. She looked on the death of her children one after the other, the recent and untimely death of her husband, the fall and destruction of her country, and the loss of all her worldly possessions. She had seen her beloved daughter Polyxena, a beautiful and innocent young girl, raped by Neoptolemus at the offerings to Achilles. Then Astyanax, the son of Hector, was thrown to his death on the rocks below, and after the death of Priam, all that was left of Ilium was a mound of rubble. Aeneas lost his wife Creusa, and with his son Ascanius and a group of Trojans, made ships and took flight to live in another land. Antenor was with them.

Hecuba, who not long before had so many sons and daughters-in-law, so many servants, was now alone in her mourning and lament, despised because she was enfeebled. Her enemies left her in solitude with no hope of aid or refuge, nor any companions or servants for consolation. There was nothing to take her eyes off the smoldering ruins. This was not the end of her prodigious calamities; for it has been told that as she was en route to Thrace and in the midst of all her anguish, the thought of Polydorus, her son, came back into her mind. He had been slaughtered by greedy Polymestor, and Hecuba recognized Polydorus' grave in the sand by the sea. This final disaster assailed her overburdened heart with such force that she was seized with a madness, howling like a dog, and in this fever she died. Others have reported that she was made a slave by the Greeks with Cassandra and Andromache, and, demented, she ended her days among them. This was the end of the king and queen, once so magnanimous and exalted. All that they had built up through the years was reduced to cinders and ashes in one day.

AGAINST THE PROUD

I wonder what they trust, all those who are not afraid to put their hope in things ephemeral? What would they think, those who are proud of their nobility, proud of their own appearance and strength, if they saw Hector dragged in the dirt and Polites dead? Were not these young noblemen handsome and valorous? Yet they rest in their graves. What do they think, who pride themselves on their children, family, and friends, when they read that Priam lay inside his own castle quivering in his blood? Who ever existed that had more brilliant children, a better family, wider lands, was richer in friends and servants? What do those wealthy ones think, with their gold, their splendid furniture and great lands, when they know that Priam was stabbed in his own palace and buried in the ruins of his homeland? Did not Priam have a great treasure? But after ten years of war there was very little to give his enemy to ransom the body of his slaughtered son or, afterward, little for a funeral or to decorate the sepulcher with gold. I am not sure, but it seems to me that unless a man has completely lost his senses, he should put aside arrogance, hollow acclaim, and foolish self-confidence, condemn his mundane work and thoughts; he should put his faith in the square gravestone in which alone lies certain strength, stability, and life eternal.

ABOUT AGAMEMNON, KING OF MYCENAE

The victorious Greek army fared little better than the Trojans they defeated.

For you who examine it carefully, the story of Priam serves as very strong proof of the power of Fortune, but you have only to read history to find its like. To really demonstrate Fortune's wide circumvolutions, let us summon Agamemnon, the general of the Greek troops, who, as a result of the fall of Priam, wished for himself a magnificent and glittering truimph. He was descended from Tantalus, whom the credulous ancients believed to be the son of Jupiter by way of Pelops and Philistenes; and by the death of Atreus and his uncle Thyestes, Agamemnon became King of Mycenae. He greatly increased his royal fame by his marriage to Clytemnestra, as some would have it daughter of Jupiter and Latona, or, as I believe more accurately, daughter of Tyndareus, King of Sparta.

When he was in Crete, he divided the treasure of Atreus with his brother. Then he heard that Helen, his brother's wife, had been seized by Paris, and quickly called the Greeks together. When they sought in vain to have Helen returned, all the Greeks who were of the same mind allied themselves against the Trojans, and appointed Agamemnon leader in the threatening war, for he was pre-eminent in the military arts and the most outstanding of all the Greeks. In fact, if we were to take into consideration the kings, the nations, the magnitude of the navy, and the duration of the conflict, we would perhaps have difficulty to discover anyone else, anywhere, at any time, engaged in so illustrious a command.

Then the enemy was conquered by strength or by skill; Agamemnon's army was enriched by the booty of Asia, and he achieved an almost immortal reputation. Ilium was destroyed, the outrage of Paris avenged by the victory, and the quarrel of Ajax and Ulysses lulled. Agamemnon assembled all the kings and allies in ships at the island of Tenedos, turned the sails into the wind, and made for the sea expecting to receive a great triumph upon his arrival in Greece. Suddenly the clouds began to darken, the sky to thunder, an impetuous wind to howl, and the sea was up-ended by a fierce hurricane. The ships were scattered. The rowers were thrown into confusion. The sails were torn away by the uproar. The sailors abandoned their posts. Nor was there yet a break. The ships, carried wherever the power of the winds drove them, began to shatter one against the other, or were crushed by rocks. What became of many of them has always remained uncertain. What can be added to

this? Between the clamor of the sailors and the vain
prayers to the gods, the members of the expedition became dispersed and confused in the dim light.

Many led astray by the treachery of Nauplius (angry
because of the unworthy death of his son) were drawn
toward the rocks of Caphareus and perished there. Some
were swallowed by the quicksands off Libya; others
were scattered among the Cyclades in the Aegean Sea;
still others found a steady wind, and these few all held
to their original destination. In this way Menelaus survived the tempest and was carried with Helen to the
kingdom of Polybus in Egypt. Mnestheus, the King of
Athens, incapacitated by sea-sickness, had put in at
Melos where he closed his days. Diomedes was driven to
the base of Mount Garganus and settled on the sea
coast of Illyricum. Ulysses was carried away by high
sea, but it is not sure exactly where.

To make a long story short, Agamemnon was in
anguish, for though victorious, he was vanquished;
though successful, subdued, and almost alone he arrived at Mycenae. The days which he hoped would be
festive, had been turned miserably into an occasion for
tears. He discovered that almost all of the kingdom was
occupied by Aegisthus, the son of Thyestes, who shamefully contaminated Agamemnon's marriage by adultery.
Agamemnon addressed himself to these problems, but
while he sought to bring destruction on his enemies and
wipe out his brother's shame, he gained only misfortune.
For a long time there was more of a war in his own
country that the one he waged among the Phrygians.
Oh happy Priam, in the midst of your children's graves
and the smoke of rubble of Troy. If your life, weighed
down by all its troubles, had endured thus far, you
would have been able to see that the vengeance for
your downfall, which the strength of Hector and the

power of the kings of Asia were unable to accomplish, was finished by a tempest of the sea, the rage of the winds, the rocks, and your enemies' own relatives.

What finally happened? Agamemnon, uncertain of the situation, feigned ignorance, and ordered that revelry be prepared while Clytemnestra planned Agamemnon's death surreptitiously. She was incited either by unhappiness—for Agamemnon had taken Cassandra as spoils of war—or by fear of punishment for the adultery she had committed; or by the affection she bore her lover. She presented Agamemnon with a robe in which there was no opening for his head, some say at supper or others as he was getting out of bed still naked. He put it on searching for an opening, and while he was encumbered in this way and could not see, he was an easy victim for Aegisthus, who was waiting for him.

He was killed at Clytemnestra's pleading, and his murderer seized the palace and all the kingdom. Alive, Agamemnon conquered Mars and Neptune with his strength, but the man who conquered others far away, in his own home was conquered by the treachery of his wife and made a human sacrifice by Aegisthus. The man who ruled kings was not able to bridle the passion of his own wife. Agamemnon felled Troy, but Aegisthus, the adulterer, felled him. Thus perfidy vanquished virtue.

POVERTY APPLAUDED

The rejection of wealth, voluntary poverty, will bring the greatest of everlasting joys.

What does great power bring with it except a covering of gold and purple, mantles and gems, the certain envy of many, the greatest misfortune, and very often a lamentable and ignominious end. Among all these things is mixed deceptive love, which brings the greatest danger to those who receive it. This delight, by the delicacies which it sets free, infects the spirit with its poison. If Troy was not enough to demonstrate this fact, how many conflagrations, how many ruins, how many killings are necessary? And in addition slaughtered Agamemnon bears witness to it.

Oh Poverty, little regarded, yet desired by many an humble person. You alone observe the laws of nature, subdue harmful cunning, eschew worldly honors, ridicule man's long sea voyage and sweaty battles. You despise superfluities. Naked, you easily withstand the summer sun, and with the greatest patience overcome the winter chill. Content in the shade of the woods you avoid the rain under this simple roof. If you are faced with hunger, you endure it with greater patience than those who endure the abundance of gold and jewels. Flitting love, secret passion, and foul seduction have all fled. You can march by the den of lions, through forests infested by robbers, safe from their treachery, and by cross-roads and towns, in the presence of the envious. Calmness, freedom, and a repose in the midst of the world is granted you. You are skillful; you are inventive; you are the distinguished mother of all laudable study. Fortune despises you, and you are equally contemptuous of her.

Why do I work so hard to enumerate your gifts? They are infinite and are all conspicuous by their goodness. If Agamemnon had eaten with you, like Xenocrates, I believe the slothful Aegisthus would scarcely have ventured against him. If Clytemnestra had been vigilant in the night to guard her home, there is no doubt she would have remained chaste rather than have become a feared adultress, and she would have earnestly desired the return of her husband.

Oh, how beautiful and sacred a thing it is to engage

in simple tasks with you; to love the country; to honor solitude, putting aside abundance to contemplate ideas celestial under the trees by silvery streams. Let others seek greatness. A small house serves me, secure with you, Diogenes, with the Roman families of Fabricius and Curius.

While I was pouring out my thoughts Samson appeared, complaining about the perfidy of his beloved wife. And so I desisted from my agreeable task and now turn my pen to the telling of his story.

ABOUT SAMSON

Samson, tricked by three different women, finally snatched victory from defeat and avenged his country like a hero.

As the facts were revealed by God through an angel, Samson was born of a certain Israelite, Manoa, and his very beautiful wife. Because he was a Nazarene, it was forbidden him by the law of God to cut his hair or to drink beer or wine, and he grew into a youth with extraordinary strength admired by everyone. The first sign of his strength appeared when, to marry a young girl whom he loved, he went into the country of the Philistines, a warlike people. A lion came into his path whom he courageously killed, but he remained silent about it. It is indicative of the magnanimous soul to impute to God the great deeds he does himself and never to reveal them in public.

Finally, as he wished to continue on his way, Samson took a honeycomb from the mouth of the beast that he had killed and ate it. He proposed a riddle to the family of the bride, offering gifts to those who could solve it. No one there could; but, induced by the charms of his wife, he revealed the secret, and was then so disturbed that he left. Because of what had happened his love turned to hate; and when he took another wife, he became an enemy of the Philistines. At the time of the next harvest, he demonstrated a new and unusual form of revenge. He had torches attached to the tails of foxes and sent them into the fields of the enemy, thus burning all their crops. This ruse angered the Philistines and, in retribution for the evil, they ordered Samson delivered to them from the Israelites. He was conveyed to them bound with ropes which he broke with the strength of his arms, grabbed the jawbone of an ass which luckily was lying there, felled and scattered the Philistines. After this feat he was very thirsty, and he saw a spring gushing from the jawbone, the work of God. Drinking from it, he was revived. This incident gave him a very great reputation among his people, and he was made a judge, which was then the name of the highest office among the Israelites. There have been those who called the lion that he killed a Nemean lion, and they thought Samson was Hercules. I do not support this view; yet I do not know anything that contradicts the testimony.

After Samson had repulsed the Philistines in this way he went into Gaza, one of their cities, and stayed at the house of a prostitute by whose charms he was enamored. Getting up during the night, he found the doors of the city tightly closed with bolts and bars in order to capture him. But he took the doors off their hinges and carried them on his shoulders to the top of a mountain which is close to Mt. Hebron.

But why is this important? These are great deeds, and they must actually be the very greatest to achieve eminence. Whoever thinks he can achieve happiness in this life, however, is foolish, for he must expect a final reckoning to all things. The man who was able to render a lion defenseless, to destroy his enemies with a jaw-bone, to tear a city gate from its hinges and to carry it to the top of a mountain, cannot prevent the slippery sport of Fortune.

For Samson had too much confidence in himself, and was overly entranced with a prostitute named Delilah, who lived with his enemies. Encouraged by a bribe, with a little dalliance and a few tears she induced him to reveal to her the cause of his great strength. Oh, Heavenly Father, just a little before he had been deceived by another woman. Now, overcome by the coaxing and false tears of a whore, the high-spirited man again allowed himself to be deceived. She was a woman truly devoted to evil, for after having been thoroughly instructed by Samson's enemies, while he was sleeping, she cut off his hair, untouched since he was born. Then she gave him, as weak as a woman, into the power of the Philistines, so they could make fun of him.

Now that Samson was without his strength, they put out his eyes, imprisoned him, and forced him, like a beast of burden, to turn the stones of a grain mill. This is what happens to a credulous person, to an amorous person, to a person who puts too much faith in a woman. Those men whom neither chains nor weapons overcame, were overcome by the tears of a woman. The man who had been the terror of his enemies, by this blow of Fortune was turned into an object of amusement.

This is a great downfall which a man with a strong spirit could not endure for long, if I am not mistaken. After a little time had passed, his hair grew back again, and the strength which was lost before now seemed to have returned. The Philistines had assembled to have a feast and make a public sacrifice to their god Dagon.

After the food had been taken off the tables, they ordered the unfortunate Samson to be brought into their presence as a joke, so they could give their festival over to merriment. He was led in by a child, and for a little while he occupied himself playfully. All the Philistines laughed at the man who was a judge of the Israelites playing in front of them. Then, as if he were tired, he had the boy lead him to the two columns on which nearly the entire roof of the temple rested and hung on them. Selecting the right moment, he grabbed them with both his hands and cried out, "Let all his enemies perish with Samson." With the miraculous strength he pulled in toward him. The pillars fell; immediately the whole edifice followed, and with Samson were destroyed all the rulers of the Philistines. Altogether the wreckage killed three thousand men. Thus the leader of the Israelites for a space of twenty years lived despised and destitute among his enemies, unable to support his life, and inflicted on himself an unworthy death.

AGAINST WOMEN

The tricks women use to capture the reason of men are many and varied.

A woman is an alluring and destructive evil, but few persons know this before they have had experience. Women have complete contempt for the laws of God; they do not try to regain the position in society from which they have been excluded because of their unfitness, but try to achieve sovereignty by a certain inborn diligence. They know that they have a bright face tinted with red and white; eyes that are large, deep, and blue; golden hair; lips that are dark red; a thin nose; a neck of ivory rising right between two round shoulders; breasts, equidistant, of some firmness, round, high, and prominent; long arms; thin hands with long fingers; a slender body, and small feet. They look after these attractions with great skill so that they can use them to get what they want. Then they consult one another, and anything about their person which seems excessive, they reduce, and any defect they patch with marvelous skill. A woman who is too thin will eat sweets and pastries, and a fat one gets thin by fasting and exercise. Women are busy keeping their curves from fading, lowering their shoulder line, bracing whatever has sagged, extending their necks, heightening themselves if short, and even correcting a limp.

What swollen hands, pimply faces, rheumy eyes, or defects in other parts I could enumerate which have all been cured without calling in the learned Hippocrates? From the same source women obtain waters to make black hair golden, curling irons to make straight hair ringed and wavy; they make their forehead higher by pulling out their hairs; eyebrows that are too big and joined together, they separate with pincers making the arc less thin. Any teeth which by chance have fallen out, they replace with ivory. What hair they cannot remove from their face with a razor, they remove with nitre, and they scrape away skin that is too thick. By these techniques they remake themselves so that if you thought before they were unattractive and shapeless, now you will think them Venus herself.

Need I mention the flowers, garlands, fillets, or coronets decked with gold and gems they decorate themselves with? It is as if they took off their clothes and dressed themselves in a little of the thinnest gold. How can I describe these clothes? These are robes glittering with gold and precious stones fit only for a king. This woman dresses herself like the Narbonnese, that one like one from the Côte d'Or, this one like the Cyprians, others like the Egyptians, Greeks, or even the Arabs. It is no longer sufficient to be dressed like an Italian.

The reason of man is blinded by feminine wiles, for women know just how to walk, just when to show a little of their alluring breasts or their legs, how they ought to use their eyes in looking at a man, what fleeting gesture will attract, what laugh is most appealing, and (this they know best) when it is the moment to show that they want what they really do not want. But how can I attempt to list their secrets? It would be easier to count the grains of sand by the seaside. I think it is more courteous to keep undisclosed how well every woman knows those mysterious, honeyed words, those enticements, those seductions, those opportune tears which men find very moving. It is by such tricks as these that the most expert observers of women are most often captured.

The person who works toward virtue finds that the object of pleasure is his greatest concern. He find that he cannot break the chain which he forged himself, and very often he is rushing to his own downfall. Woe is me! Isn't the natural beauty of a young woman enough to bring about the fall of the human race without the addition of all these mysteries? The first man, perhaps, was captured by them. Paris, Aegisthus, and Samson were all captured by them and by these snares. The great Hercules was seized to serve as an example to other mortals. He not only forgot Deianira, whom he loved very much, but was also unmindful of his tremendous reputation when he made himself subservient to the orders of a young girl. He put aside the exercise of manly strength and took on the duties of a housewife. Iole had been able to accomplish all this on such a man by artifices: the wink of her eye, the beauty and grace of her figure. And, what is even worse, Hercules was affected not in the age when the flames of passion burn most strongly, but when he was an old man.

To be sure, the female of the species is very greedy, quick to anger, unfaithful, oversexed, truculent, desirous more of frivolity than of wisdom. If I am lying, then their deeds will make them known. For money, Delilah gave Samson over to his enemies; Eriphyle, because she wanted a necklace, revealed where Amphiaraus was hiding. On her lap Danae received Jupiter who had turned into gold and flowed down through the roof. Arachne hanged herself when she was overcome by Pallas. Amata, too, hanged herself when she learned Aeneas was victorious, as did Phyllis, impatient for the love of Demophoon. With whom should Nisus, King of Megara, have believed himself more safe than Scylla? But she, a mistress to passion, betrayed both her father and her country to the enemy. Where should Agamemnon have been more secure than in the arms of his wife? But she, blinded by the flames of adultery, delivered him up to be killed. I will put aside as a joke the infamous law of Semiramis, but Hercules was seduced by the alluring Iole, Solomon by the Egyptian, Antony by Cleopatra. Medea plundered her father, dismembered her brother, and did not spare her own children. Procne not only killed her son, Itys, but also prepared him as a meal for her husband.

Young men, do not let me give you any more examples but go ahead, let women capture you like blind men with their snares. Embroil yourselves with these creatures, so true, so loyal, so kind! Follow your own advice, and believe what women tell you. If there are those among you who say Samson was not strong, that Hercules was not captured by a little girl to be remembered by posterity as a servant, that women are not all as bad, I will not teach you the difference. However, I want you to judge if you could have overthrown Anthaeus or killed Diomedes, or conquered Geryones, with its three bodies, or led Cerberus away, or whether, with great and persevering determination, you could ever have overcome Hercules himself, even if he was weakened by love. We could never equal his labors. Circes could not deceive Ulysses with her potion, nor could the song of the Sirenes detain him, nor the danger of the sea terrify him.

No man can conquer others who has not first conquered himself. Therefore, if you will control the unrestrained passion which you have within you, then women will set their net and try their wiles in vain. Even if they have the grace to want children (which is not often the case), it is not necessary to be their slaves. If we are truly men, we have to show why we love women. It is not in any way necessary to divide the power given us with them, much less to abdicate to them, as a few persons overly devoted to women have done to their great disaster. It is not necessary to believe a woman's tears or her complaints, but a person should be as wary of their cunning as of that of an implacable foe.

I am not convinced that all women are artful; for who does not believe that among so great a number you might find some who are dutiful, modest, very holy, and worthy of the highest respect? I will not mention the Christian women who have a high reputation for magnanimity, integrity, virginity, simplicity, chastity, constancy, and other virtues, but some pagans who merit the highest praise. And if I ever meet them, I will have to love, honor, and extol them beyond any man for their

virtues. Herculean strength is more admirable in one
of the Pygmaei than in Briareus,[1] and more commendable
in woman than in man—but how very rare! But I flee
them all after paying this debt to posterity; for hunting
a Lucretia, you will stumble upon a Calpurnia or a
Sempronia.[2]

SOME MORE IN MISERY

*The author dismissed some complainers so he could
rest at the end of the book.*

I had written enough against the desire of women
and those who carry love to foolish extremes when I
heard the noise of people weeping. Among them was
Pyrrhus, the son of Achilles. After the capture of Troy
and a meandering voyage over the sea, he took up the
life of a pirate. He gave Andromache to Helenus and he
married Hermione, but because of the deceit of Macareus
he was killed by Orestes in the temple of Apollo at
Delphi. After him came Evander, complaining in a
tremulous voice, his beard snarled, dirty, and sparse,
his clothes ripped. He cursed his old age because his
only son, Pallas, had been slaughtered.

Although, to be sure, I was born to work, still I am
not made of iron, and I was weary with writing. I
thought I would take a little rest. Since the work is
under way, I would like to divide it into books, and here
I want to bring the first book to a close. I have not
considered the progress of all the books, yet there is
some diversity between the preceding subjects and those
that are to follow which can fitly be separated according

[1] A hundred-armed giant.
[2] Suspected of poisoning her own husband.

to the general intention. We shall follow the practice of travelers who make their way through a wide-open landscape. They divide the road into separate stretches, marked now by a stone, now by an old oak, now by a small chapel or a clear fountain, stream, or river which flows across the path. In this way they more easily measure their progress, what has gone past and what is yet to come, and they are able to point out their experiences more clearly. In the same way, instead of going along without any stops, we shall make a brief delay, leaving our mark whenever we are tired and come to a landmark of an outstanding experience. This is what we mean by the end of this book. By means of such boundaries as this, readers are more likely to be pleased by the hope of what is to come, and can more easily remember what they wish.

A SHORT INTRODUCTION

There are those who say that perhaps we now have
enough examples to demonstrate the strength of Fortune,
how unstable are earthly things, how false the hope of
happiness, how empty is fame, and that this sufficiency
makes anything more superfluous. As for me, I suggest
that no single example be omitted which might move a
human spirit toward the right path. But I undertook this
task not for this alone. There are many who rely on
things that are transitory. They scarcely feel the constantly roaring wind, and, of course, they do not hear
words spoken quietly. These people, I think, should always be continually hit with the blows of impressive
examples. As a constant flow of water will penetrate
the hardest stone, so an adamantine heart is softened
by a long narration. And to those whom these examples
suffice, I give thanks that I have worked thus far with
their good grace. But I shall continue to satisfy the
others.

AGAINST THE PRESUMPTUOUS
PRIDE OF KINGS

*The king derives his power from his people and
should be their father, not their tyrant.*

People should not be threatened with force, trampled
underfoot, nor tortured. Rulers should always remember
that people are not slaves but fellow servants of God.

Because it is the sweat of the people that makes the royal eminence shine, the king should be diligent to guard peace and welfare of the people. How rulers perform this today, God knows. Rule has been transformed into tyranny. Rulers despise the feelings of their subjects. They want to glitter with gems and gold; they want to be surrounded by great bands of servants, to build palaces into the sky, to spend their time with groups of parasites, prostitutes and fools. They feast their eyes on obscenities. They spend their nights in endless debauchery, drunkenness, and scandal. Their days they pass in the deepest sleep while the people guard their well-being.

They make wars, not justly, but in reprisal for personal injury. Believing themselves infallible, they reject the counsel of the wise and believe only themselves. They put aside whatever is good and take up whatever is evil. They burden the city with taxes, torture the citizens, exile and massacre them, trample them into the mud under their feet.

What shameful wickedness! How dishonorable and disgraceful the depravity of these thieves and gluttons— I will not call them kings. How patient and long-suffering the people. How senseless and stupid the self-confidence of rulers. They think that while they sport, the people will be faithful and obedient to them. I ask you when I see those to whom I would grant all my respect, should I call him king of liberty, dignity, duty, and everything I hold dear? Whose command do I obey? For whom do I labor, to whom do I give part of my property, for whose safety do I spill my blood? He watches over me with destruction, desolation, and insult, and when he is thirsty, he sucks my blood. His great skill, with which he ought to sustain the poor and unfortunate, he wastes on prostitutes, entertainers, and

other such pariahs. I see him rely on the worst of counsels and admire the worst deeds, but regarding the
public welfare he is sluggish, torpid, and dull.

Shall I call him king? Shall I venerate him as a prince?
Shall I keep faith as if he were the Lord? Hardly. He
is an enemy. To conspire against this kind of ruler, to
take up arms, to deceive, to oppose this man is an act
of greatness and, even more, of necessity. Scarcely any
offering is more acceptable to God than the blood of a
tyrant. He who returns evil for good is harsh and intolerable. The kings may contradict it as much as they
wish, even deny it a hundred times, but still they rule
only by the support of their subjects, and the people's
strength makes them formidable. When any king unjustly weakens the people by slaughter or injuries, at
once he feels his power diminish.

But whom do I call the people? This lowest class
should be not despised. Anyone who is wounded carries
a great soul within his breast. The life of every ruler,
protected by a bodyguard, cannot be reckoned any more
durable than the life of anyone willing to lose his own
life to kill that king. Mucius Scaevola all alone got well
within the camp of the Etruscans; and because he had
great courage, he would have killed the king, Porsenna,
in the midst of the king's own army, if he had been able
to recognize him. Extraordinary men have dared the
greatest deeds, and what they have dared, they have
accomplished. Junius Brutus turned the Roman people
against Tarquin the Proud, Virginius against Appius
Claudius, The Decemvir. Pausanias slaughtered Philip,
King of Macedonia, in the presence of his son and
father-in-law. A single slave killed Hasdrubel, the famous leader of the Carthaginians.

Why should I enumerate so many, when these are
well known without any further examples? Therefore

those who wish to rule others, if they desire a long reign and the lasting faith of the people, should learn to suppress their desires and bridle their passions; but the most sacred law is to be loved rather than feared. To the people they rule they should seem fathers rather than emperors.

ABOUT DIDO, QUEEN OF CARTHAGE

*Dido led her people to a promised land but
could never forget her dead husband.*

I put my other work aside for I saw Dido of Tyre coming, to whom, perhaps, Fortune had done injury, for I saw she was dressed as she had been on the last day of her life when she ascended her funeral pyre. Although her face was calm and pale, it was lined with tears as she bemoaned her fate.

You will find the name of scarcely any nation as celebrated as that of the Phoenicians, if any trust can be put in the writings of the ancients. After they occupied the shore of Syria, they embellished the place with their natural and praiseworthy skills, and the fame of what they did spread over the whole western world.

It is generally believed that after the death of King Belus, who had descended from their ancient rulers, Pygmalion, his son, took the throne. His daughter, Elissa, afterward called Dido, was an outstanding beauty, and she was given in marriage to Acerbas, or Sichaeus as others say, her maternal uncle and a priest of Hercules, who was the first citizen of Tyre, later their king. A handsome man, he was greatly respected by his people, and was loved by his wife whom he in turn loved deeply.

Now the cause of the downfall of this once happy woman was worldly wealth, thought by many to be the source of almost all happiness. Acerbas abounded in riches, for which Pygmalion, very avaricious, burned with desire; and he thought that by the death of Acerbas he could easily get them all for himself. So he kill Acerbas, taking him by surprise. Dido took the death of her husband very grievously, and for a long time she mourned, crying inconsolably, and continually cursed her brother.

With the passing of time her unhappiness abated somewhat, and misery gave way to reason. She thought about Pygmalion's insatiable avarice, and, warned in a dream, she began to fear him and to realize that her only safety lay in flight. She communicated this idea to certain princes whom she knew had little reason to love the king, and convinced them of her opinion. Then with feminine cunning she fooled her brother into giving her ships. She told him that she could live in her husband's house no longer because she was disturbed too much by his constant memory; against her will it remained fresh, for all the time she had to look at the rooms where she once saw her beloved Acerbas. If, for this reason, Pygmalion would send her ships and sailors, she would gladly return to her own country with everything Acerbas had owned.

Pygmalion, who had once sought what was now offered to him, was happy. Very willingly he sent the ships which would have the honor of bringing his sister back. Dido thought she would overcome trickery by trickery. She secreted all of her husband's great treasure on the ships, and in their place in plain sight she put money-bags full of sand. In the early evening she set sail with her own company as well as with the envoys of the king. When she was far at sea, she ordered the bags thrown into the sea. Then in tears she thus addressed the group:

"My beloved traveling companions! You do not understand what you have just done. You have thrown the wealth of Acerbas and Pygmalion into the waves, and in this way I have made friends either for death or for flight. You are certainly familiar with the avarice of Pygmalion. Because of these riches he killed my husband. There is no doubt that if we now go to him, disappointed in his hope for this wealth and exceedingly angry since he has seen the riches thrown away, he will torture and kill all of us. I would surrender to that willingly after losing the man I loved so much, but I have a regard for you, and for that reason, if you want me to flee from my nefarious brother, I shall spare my life, and with good luck shall lead you to a happier place."

They were moved both by their fear of the savage king and by the eloquence of Dido's oration; and though it was hard for them to leave their native land, they immediately turned their ships from Tyre toward Cyprus. Here Dido received a priest of Jupiter with his wife and children, and he made a favorable prediction for the future trip. She did not know, however, where she ought to go so the young men would not become old without children. Therefore she rounded up seventy girls who were there on the shore. According to an old custom of the Cyprians they had gathered to mate with any travelers. In this way they acquired a dowry for any future marriage, and afterward would give sacrifices to Venus for their subsequent modesty.

After the Tyrians had been at sea again for some time, they guided their ships to the shore of Africa, and from the inhabitants there they bought as much land as could be surrounded by the hide of a bull. For a strategem, however, they sliced the hide in small pieces like parchment and cut the pieces up lengthwise. In this way they were able to occupy more of the land than the Africans had thought possible. Then, while her weary companions refreshed themselves, Dido repaired the vessels, and those that were especially suitable she ordered restored.

Some of the inhabitants of the surrounding area came to help carry the Tyrian goods to the shore and others came to look at the strangers, to make conversation, to enter into trade, and to make friends. When Dido and her people considered this phenomenon as well as the comforts of the place, it seemed advisable to end their flight here, so she revealed the treasure of Acerbas to them and aroused in them the highest hopes for the future.

Where they were digging for the foundation of the city, they discovered the head of a horse, demonstrating that the place was advantageous. Dido surrounded all the land that they had purchased with a wall and called the place Carthage, from the word *cartha,* a sheet of parchment, according to some. Their fortress they called Byra, from the hide of a bull, which in the Tyrian language is *byrsa.* After a short time this city increased in population because of its very favorable situation, and here, making the laws, queenly Dido ruled with complete justice. She lived as a very honorable widow, observing the sacred virtue of chastity. And she thus achieved her desire. She had lived in Tyre in great misery, but in Africa her wonderful reputation for virtue blossomed. From this example, it is apparent to everyone that reputations are not kept bright in one's own home. Many are held back by their own cowardice, and, surrounded by a dark cloud, they die unknown to others as if they had never lived, and like smoke vanish into the air.

However, Fortune (always impatient when the conditions of life are joyful) placed something both very

powerful and shaky under the feet of this chaste queen.
What should have resulted in a brighter glory and esteem
brought on a death worthy of compassion. Dido's reputation for beauty, honor, and prudence increased, and
the fame of her kingdom spread to the most remote
peoples. The King of Maxitana, a town near hers, burned
fervently for her love. He called some of the nobles of
Carthage to him and sought from them his marriage
with the queen. Unless it was given him he threatened
to destroy completely both the city and its people.
The nobles knew about the queen's inflexible resolution
to remain chaste, and did not dare tell her of the king's
threat directly. Therefore with Punic astuteness they told
the queen that the King of Maxitana wanted someone
from her court who could instruct him in the customs
and life of the Tyrians, but they did not know anyone
suitable for this task. There was no one who wanted to
leave his own country for so monstrous a king living so
barbarously. If no one would go, however, war would
follow, and so great danger hung over the city. Sharply
the queen rebuked them and said:

"Let us put aside our life to work among the savages
and barbarians. If it is necessary to die for the salvation
of your country, as good citizens are you not prepared
for that? It is only a bad citizen who is afraid to give
up his personal comforts for the good of the homeland."
Then the nobles revealed the commission of the king,
believing she had been convinced of the marriage by
her own words. She recognized that what she actually
had said had been contrary to her resolution to remain
chaste, and for a long time she called on the name of
Acerbas in tears and lamentation.

Finally she promised that she would go to her husband
as the fates directed her. She took the space of three
months to accomplish the wishes of the king and of

her subjects. During this time, I believe, if anything was lacking to strengthen the defense of the city, this she supplied very quickly so that no part of the city she built was unfortified. Realizing what was going to happen she endlessly cursed her beauty, endlessly cursed envious fortune and all that had occurred. The result of frustrating the avarice of her brother, of the successful flight, of founding a great city, and of gathering together a numerous people was anxiety, tears, and misery.

That time of year had returned when again she periodically celebrated the death of Acerbas, and she ordered that a huge pyre be constructed in the highest part of the city as if she would placate his soul. She had some sacrifices made, then took a blade, and, mounting the pyre in the sight of the people, she spoke:

"Oh, great citizens, as you commanded, I am going to my husband," and right there she fell upon the sword. Having saved her honor and chastity, she stained all the surroundings with her innocent blood. When the Carthaginians saw this frightful deed, they wept, bemoaning the great and pure queen. Celebrating the funeral with great mourning they called on Dido, the mother of their country, extending all honors, human and divine, to her. The good, which in her lifetime the cruelty of Fortune had taken from her, in her death the respect of her citizens returned to her. Enthusiastically they entrusted her to their gods, and while Carthage remained unconquered, they erected altars and temples dedicated to her name, revering her as a goddess.

IN PRAISE OF DIDO

Oh, the strength of this woman! Oh, the honor of womanly chastity which should be perpetually praised!

To preserve your virtue, Dido, you preferred to give to fate those few years which remained of your life rather than to ask for a longer time if it had to be lived in shame, or if it meant soiling holy chastity with the smear of desire that is both a trap and indelible. Truly with one blow you, venerable queen, put an end to mortal travail and achieved immortal fame. Truly you restrained the license of the barbarian king, and by extinguishing your spark of life, you saved your undefended country from war. Truly your very chaste spirit spread your renown and your nobility, and by your merits your illustrious soul flew to the life prepared for you.

Therefore I pray you, if your soul has some power among the gods, that by your deed you inspire modesty in licentious women, that after so many centuries they may acknowledge your name with honor, and that we can see the growth of respect for chastity in marriage.

ABOUT SARDANAPALUS
KING OF ASSYRIA

*Only after he had lost his kingdom did this king
realize the cost of indolence and luxury.*

I was still thinking about Dido's consecration, when the hubbub of people weeping assailed my ears. I turned to them and saw a great column coming toward me. The line of notables was led by Sardanapalus, the last King of the Assyrians, not perfumed nor dressed in shining purple robes, but scorched in appearance, bearing the signs of the fire that killed him. I decided to write the story of his voluptuous life with its cycle of fortune for those who think good fortune is stable and everlasting because with one ruler it continued for a short time. Fortune wished for a change after she had drawn him from the very bowels of the earth.

By the death of Ocrasapes, the thirty-fifth King of the Assyrians, Sardanapalus, whom the Assyrians call Tonosconcoter, inherited the kingdom that his ancestors had acquired after great difficulties. Toward the beginning of his reign, after he had founded the cities of Tarsus and Ancale, he withdrew into his palace filled with wondrous delights. Growing lazy from idleness, he discovered many new kinds of luxury, it is believed. People say that he invented the bed covered with soft feathers decorated with silk covers, and enclosed by screens on every side. In addition he introduced drinking cups of gold and gems, banquets prepared with special skill, wines pressed by other means than feet, perfumes and ointments which provoke desire, and ranks of servants beautifully appareled. Phoroneus, it has been said, achieved everlasting fame for having established law; Saturn demonstrated agriculture to the unskilled Italians; Erichthonius invented the four-horse chariot; but Sardanapalus, master and originator of debauchery and sloth, had not yet discovered that the fame of those three would be obscured by his accomplishments. They did not discover the dissolute life.

After Sardanapalus turned over the care of his kingdom to his prefects, he withdrew from the sight of all his subjects, as if this would increase his majesty. But do not think that he was condemned to solitary confinement, for he sought out friends: cooks smelling of the kitchen, butchers stained with blood of their meat, fishmongers covered with the scales of their fish. The most dangerous kinds of men, flatterers and entertainers, were present continuously feasting then belching forth the drunkenness of the day before. There were also those

whom he especially preferred, panderers from the bor-
dellos, the scum of all others—and, in fact, all the masters
of sensuality and corruption. To these the palace was
always open and the court was a public hall. Finally, to
perfect this association in lasciviousness, they added
numerous women to their group.

No other shepherd had such a suitable flock. This
celebrated king revelled in sumptuous and continuous
entertainments. Often the carousal extended through the
best part of the day and most of the night. Then, satiated
with wines and sauces, the king left the feast and went
into small rooms and places hidden from view where
he put aside his restraint and engaged prostitutes for
the greatest perversions. What diversions, what sensa-
tions, and what practices and what words passed I have
never heard nor do I surmise. If I had heard, good taste
would prevent me from revealing them. Let me say only
that it would not be fitting to discuss what they did even
in the midst of a house of prostitution among the panderers and whores.

After taking his pleasure, so shamefully besotted, enfeebled, and exhausted, Sardanapalus fell into a sleep
which extended from the night into the height of the
day. When he got up, because he had come into the
company of kings and nobles, he dressed himself in
kingly fashion. He put on a golden belt and decorated
himself like a woman. He soaked his beard with oil
from India, and when he made laws for his people, he
sat on a golden throne in the midst of women spinning.
He handled the thread, laid out the wool, and, his fingers
sparkling with the splendour of a variety of precious
stones, he performed all the tasks of a woman without
embarrassment.

Oh, the laudable duties of a king! Oh, the panorama
of conquering the enemy! See a king carrying a spindle

among the servant girls! What then? Who does not doubt that the king sometimes put down the spindle to deal with the arduous tasks of the kingdom and to give his counsel to his venerable senate? Or that, living among concubines he directed the prefects of his provinces, the leaders of his army, his military tribunes and commanders as well as his collectors of revenues according to the judgment of these women? For a price he gave them the blood of men and the souls of his subjects, freeing malefactors from death and torture and ruling everything according to their pleasure.

Oh, happy Assyrians! Instead of a single king, a college of remarkable queens watched over you continuously. So that the king wasted none of his time, if he were not occupied with feasts, lust, sleep, and palaver, he turned to his company of parasites and buffoons. Here there was no discussion concerning the deeds of outstanding men, the virtues of holy men, the sacred doctrines of philosophy. They exulted over their scandalous practices, they urged sensuality, commended ignominy, and condemned all those who lived honorably. In such a manner Sardanapalus spent all the days of his life, according to the belief of most of his own people and the most propitious belief of those of today.

Then, after he had reigned so unfruitfully to his twentieth year, it seemed grievous to Fortune that one so slothful and depraved should be thought happy and should remain in this state; therefore she inspired Arbactus, who was the leader of the Medes, to deliberate with Sardanapalus concerning some very serious affairs. On a certain day, Arbactus was able to get an audience, although only with great difficulty. He saw the king sitting in the midst of his flock, weaving a cloth and acting like a servant for the women. Offended, Arbactus returned to his post and then made the degradation of Sardanapalus known. He announced that he would no

longer obey the effeminate king, and when he had converted the Medes to this opinion, he resolved that he
would make war immediately on the slothful monarch.

Sardanapalus, however, perceived this plan before it
was shown to him, and, putting down his spindle, he
aroused himself a little to take up arms. I will not deny
what is possible. His army was made up of the panderers, the gluttons, and the flatterers. Inflated by their
stories, he did not think that he was Sardanapalus fighting the Medes but Jupiter fighting the giants. The Medes,
however, did not receive him with wine, sweet talk, and
caresses, but with real swords and a cavalry prepared
and armed. Without waiting, Sardanapalus fled the battle
and retreated into his palace. Trembling, he sought
refuge in the arms of his mistresses. From there, he saw
victorious Arbactus move his army ever closer.

At last he awoke from the torpor of his long and
dulling sleep. He opened the eyes of his understanding
and saw that there was no way by which he could
recover the time that had slipped away. For the future
nothing remained but slavery or death. He put aside
his womanly spirit, put on the aspect of a man, and,
preferring death to slavery, tried to seize what he could
from an adverse fortune. In the midst of the great hall
he built a pyre. First he threw all his precious goods on
it, then mounted it himself. To those who were there he
gave his last order—one that did not come from his
former dissolute life. He ordered that on his tomb these
words be enscribed: "All that sensuality gave me, I now
possess; all that nobility possessed, I leave behind." Then
he set the fire to his durable spirit which consumed his
life and licentiousness alike. He who had led the life of a
woman, by the adversity of fortune died like a man. He
left his kingdom, which for twelve hundred years had
ruled Asia, under the rule of the Medes.

AGAINST SARDANAPALUS
AND HIS ILK

*One who spends his life in sloth and pleasure,
might as well never have lived.*

Oh, wise king, skilfully watching over the commonweal!
How well you distributed your time and work among
women, revelry, sleep, and fornication, contributing to
each in turn! It is enough that you showed us only time
is ours; all the rest belongs to Fortune. You dispensed
your time in notorious behavior so that you would not
waste it in sloth. I pray you, oh king, what is more un-
fruitful than to waste time in idleness—which you wanted
more than anything else—or to wear it away in lascivious
activity.

We are glad to be born, and with all our soul we
hope, and we will try, to extend our life into a long old
age. There is a great difference between enduring for
a very long time to delight in pleasure, and enduring
to strive ardently that we might make our fame known
through a great many centuries. But as you, Sardanapalus, lived in permanent disgrace, so you worked lascivi-
ously and shamefully. He spent his time well who copied
the *Iliad* of Homer on a thin parchment in small letters
to enclose it in the shell of a tiny nut. Callicrates spent
his time well, also, when the ants he carved from ivory
achieved a unique magnitude. And Mermecides, too,
when from the same material he carved chariots and four
horses so small that a fly could hide them with its
wings, and a ship that a small bee concealed in the
same manner. These accomplishments were neither use-

less nor shameful, for though these statuettes were made of useless material, they gave proof of great genius to all posterity. Pythagoras' life was much better still. While he traveled over the surface of the earth, he examined many different objects, learning about them so that future life and knowledge were very much advanced. Plato is still another example, as well as Apollonius and the men who sweated in arms on fields of battle—like Miltiades, Leonidas, Epaminondas, the Scipios, and other great men. These gave honor and everlasting fame to their countries. But you, Sardanapalus, are the dishonor of kings, cooing in the arms of your servant girls and exercising your passions to exhaustion. In this way you passed the hours you could never regain.

What man is more indecent than one who forgets himself as a slave to wine and revelry? The man who squanders his time in drunkenness is not the man who uses his ingenuity to discover the wines and sauces of which you, Sardanapalus, were a great devotee. It is more likely the man whose diet is acorns and water. The manner in which man lives and eats is differentiated from that of the animals by his use of moderation. But you dreaded moderation. So that you might spend your time slavishly, you ordered a surfeit brought into your presence. Then you licked up so much that it seemed you were insatiable. So all your cups would overflow, you demanded encouragement from those who were present.

And what should be more condemned than copious sleeping? To give up time to sleep is to lose it. With too much sleeping the spirit becomes dull, the memory lax, the arms and legs stiff with too much fluid. Those who are given to excessive sleep become lazy. This excess is contrary to the nature of most persons, but for those who have been given public or private trust, it

is the greatest of mortal dangers. Oftentimes kingdoms
or great persons were in a difficulty which could otherwise have been overcome, but by the inactivity of sleep
both were reduced to poverty. How much harm did
this king do with his sloth and flattery? And you who
have kept your ears carefully open to these lofty senti-
ments, have now heard enough.

A FEW THOUGHTS ABOUT DREAMS

*How certain kinds of dreams foretell events,
and a few well known examples.*

I beg of you, which of these two ideas should be regarded with more astonishment: the tremendous, almost
permanent necessity of fate, or its very certain proof in
dreams? It is, of course, apparent that God Himself, Who
sees all events as if they were in the present, with His
living voice would be able to tell what will take place
even to those who are awake. However, there is a certain
divine something implanted in the souls of men; when
the body is asleep, this something is released by our
thoughts and is less imprisoned by the solidity of the
body. It is then that we hear and see the things that
will take place either in actual visions or under the veil
of allegory.

I would not believe this had I not long since become
convinced of it by the many visions of famous persons.
The dream of the poet Simonides has been sufficiently
attested. While he was sleeping, the dead body of a
man he had seen the day before was revealed to him.
He was prevented from making a sea voyage he had
planned, for he heeded the dream and then learned that
the ship on which he would have sailed was destroyed

by a storm. If Julius Caesar had believed the dream of his wife Calpurnia, he would not have been felled by the hands of the conspirators on that very day. Augustus Caesar, too, believing what Artorious had learned from Minerva in a dream, avoided being killed in his own camp by Cassius. And Atterius would have lived longer if he had believed a dream where he saw himself wishing to leave the theater at Syracuse, rather than believe those who persuaded him to remain.

What more can I say? If we do not believe what pagans have written, then at least we ought to believe divine scripture. Here we have the story of the Pharaoh of Egypt who saw the seven lean cattle devour the seven fat cattle. We know that this was interpreted by Joseph to mean that seven years of plenty about to come would be followed by a famine. So also the King of Babylon in a dream saw some axes that cut the roots of a very tall tree. From this he was advised by Daniel about his future downfall. I cannot run through all such cases, for there is an infinite number of examples which clearly show the validity of dreams. Of course, no one must believe that every time he dreams there is a divine communication, or that each dream is a present from God. For many reasons a man's spirit is frequently led into confusing obscurities. Therefore even if one puts complete faith in dreams, they cannot always be believed. As in everything, above all one should carefully weigh between rejecting a dream or believing it. In that way we will not neglect anything that is for our benefit, nor, on the other hand, will we be disturbed by something harmless.

AN INVECTIVE AGAINST DECEIT

Deceit is truly the worst kind of evil, for with a pleasing face, honeyed words, a humble step, she is ever watchful to snare the pure in faith. And to inject her poisonous sting she invokes the name of God often for frivolous purposes. She is so strong, so clever, so artful that she overthrows the venerable power of the law. She deceives the wisdom of man and conquers the power of arms. She beguiles any skill and very often confounds any vigilance. The most shamefully evil men, and those without any principles make great use of her, for she has no constancy of virtue or strength of mind. Beneath her cloak of honor she always carries snares, lures and craftiness. She tramples the simple and credulous under her feet and frequently brings them to ruin with her sham. She uses her poison on those who would inject it in another. This is what happened to Metius. Contrary to his promise and a firm treaty sworn to by his religion, he secretly tried to separate the Albans from the Roman rule but accomplished instead the public mutilation of his body. Therefore, let Metius bemoan the fate he so deserved.

Now we put an end to this book, and for a little while we can rest.

INTRODUCTION

Those who take long and fatiguing trips not only stop sometimes to mop their brow, to rest their legs, to catch their breath, to quench their thirst, but also they turn around to measure how far they have gone. They call to mind again the towns, rivers, mountains, valleys, and seas they have crossed. Thus, by reviewing the trip that has passed, they renew their strength for the remainder of their effort.

In the same way, after a little while I turned myself around, and with the most careful reflection I began to gather our personages together and wonder especially by what ways, what powers, what causes they were all overthrown. It seemed to me, if I am not deceived, that for the most part they called their adverse fortune down on themselves. I have found the essence of a fable I remember hearing as a young man to be true. And it does not seem inappropriate in our present situation, while we are resting, to tell it.

THE FIGHT OF POVERTY
AND FORTUNE

*Poverty overthrows Fortune and
wins a promise from her.*

When I was still a youth in Naples, I studied with a Negro from Genoa—Andalo—a famous and respected master who taught us about the movements of the stars

and of the planets. One day, reading to us as usual, he
came upon these words: "Do not blame the stars when
the fallen bring about their own misfortune." Although
our teacher was old, he still had a sense of humor. Smiling at us, he spoke:

"This truth can actually be proved by a very ancient
and pleasant little tale." The men listening to him, both
those who were famous noblemen and I, pleaded with
him to tell it to us. He was of an affable and tolerant
nature, and immediately began to relate it eloquently.

"Poverty was seated at a crossroad dressed in patched
clothing, her eyes lowered, as was her custom, for she
was turning over many things in her mind. By chance
Fortune passed that way and saw her. When Fortune
laughed at her, Poverty got up and with a serious expression asked:

" 'Why are you laughing, fool?'

" 'At you, skinny, scurvy, sallow, and scaly, in a
threadbare cloak, half-covered with torn rags. Without
friends, wherever you go you bring out the dogs. Living
alone, the shame of your extremity doesn't upset you.'

"Poverty was provoked by this, and, hardly restrain-
ing her fists, she said:

" 'If you think that I am foolish because of anything
you do, you are wrong. I act of my own free will. But
let us put these things aside. Your skin is well-filled,
soft, and sanguine. You are dressed in rich clothes and
are followed by a long line of servants. How would you
like to test your strength against me in a fight?'

"Fortune had been laughing, but stopped:

" 'How stubborn this miserable creature is. We have
reduced her to the worst condition of the world, yet so
far we haven't been able to smother her pride. By
Gemini, you imitation of the tomb, if you don't be quiet,

I'll bury you in the depths of Hell with that foolish dream of yours.'

"Poverty was a little more excited:

" 'Already we have won some of the victory,' she said. 'Our cause progresses. This huntress is disturbed.' Then she added, 'Perhaps you think I am going to flatter you to soothe you. Hardly. That's how you usually think. You have never beaten me with that. Of my own free will I have given up everything of yours, and against your will I have gained the whole world for myself. I speak to you as a free woman, not your slave. When you thought that you would throw me into Hell by your tricks, without knowing it, you raised me to Heaven. Go address your threats to kings. Although my skin is pale and I am quiet in spirit, I am still forceful. Rather than fearing your threats, I'll even put them down, if I wrestle against you.'

"Fortune now lost her patience with these words:

" 'You filthiest creature, I test my strength against yours? I, who have conquered giants and overthrown emperors? If you keep talking, I will swing you round my little finger and throw you off the top of the Rhiphaeian mountains.'

Then Poverty said:

" 'I'd like to put in a good word. I believe you do great things. Joyfully, I have often observed what you say. But frightened I have never been. Leaving out the threats of injuries, do you want to do what I said? You should not reject the idea if you have conquered kings. As for me, I was nurse of the Roman Empire; nor was I covered with a better cloak than I am now.'

"Fortune, almost desperate, said:

" 'This whore is really trying to drive me crazy with her presumption. I didn't make it clear how dangerous it is to make me angry. Now get ready, world-famous nurse, for I am coming. In what kind of match, oh great offspring of Hercules, do you want to demonstrate your strength?'

"Immediately Poverty answered:

" 'I have neither shield, lance, helmet, breastplate, nor charger. I have to fight on foot. This is the condition I lay down, that whoever wins, can impose what law she wants on the other.'

"Then Fortune laughed and said:

" 'I know that you travel light. You've been a long time getting your bindle together. Yet I don't trust you very much, for it seems to me you've left it with a friend. But who will we have see the fight and judge it? We are going to fight according to this agreement; if I win, how will I impose any conditions on you that you will obey, since you do not have anything? If I wish, I could take all the wealth away from Darius or the empire from Alexander of Macedonia. In the same way I can condemn you to misery even if you aren't miserable now. But what are you going to give to me, since you don't have any friends or relatives?'

" 'You act as if you had already won,' Poverty answered. 'But it is I who is to be victorious. I don't ask anything of you but your word, which isn't worth much, really. But I will allow myself to be bound in chains, if all else fails, and that is enough for you.'

"Fortune laughed even more, then replied:

" 'I will lead you in triumph before my chariot as I led Assuerus, the most famous king of kings. And if I imprison you, I will take care of your starved and weakened hide at my expense. But what good does all this do? I will commit you to the tortures of Hell.'

"Fortune ran at Poverty, waving her arms as if she

would pound her into the center of the earth. But Poverty was ready and blocked Fortune with her elbows. Then she spun Fortune around in the air and finally threw her to the ground. Then Poverty pushed her knee into Fortune's chest and pressed her other foot into her neck. Fortune struggled for breath, but Poverty did not permit her to get up until she confessed herself beaten and until she swore an oath that she would faithfully observe the conditions agreed upon before the fight. Victorious Poverty got up and allowed herself some rest, for she was somewhat tired and exhausted. Then she said:

" 'Now that you see what my strength can do against you, you will be more careful after this about laughing when you see me. If you don't, you will be flogged. And now that you know my strength, I want you to know my kindness, though you don't deserve it. I think I would enjoy breaking your wheel and returning you to a private life. Being merciful, however, I only want you to observe this law. In your judgment—which it seems was an error of the ancients—you can raise up and bring both success and failure. I wish on my own to remove the means of your power from you, and I command that you make Misfortune fast to a stake in public, and you make him secure with chains, so that he is not only unable to go into anyone's home, but also cannot go from there unless he goes with the person who released his bonds. You can send Good Fortune where you want. Then you will be free from the conditions that were made.'

"Wonderful to say, what never happened before nor will ever happen again, Fortune kept her pledge to Poverty, it is said, and left Misfortune attached to a post for those only who would release her. By means of this

old fable you young men can understand easily what
before could not have been readily proved to the slow
of learning."

This story was received pleasurably by all those who
heard Andalo. I think this fable is acceptable if, with
the keenness of our mind, we wish to consider the customs of mankind and the judgment of God. But just
then many of those who released Misfortune from the
stake called to me in their torment.

ABOUT TULLUS HOSTILIUS AND
TARQUIN THE ELDER

A few early kings of Rome, and some of their difficulties.

I had it in mind to return to Asia, but the clamor of
some Italians called me into Italy, where I did not want
to go. For a long time the Latin people had remained
uncultivated, since their desires were few and trifling.
Later, however, they wished to increase their power,
and disastrously they began to change their kings and
to suffer with the unhappiness they had not previously
experienced. And as fire seems warmer to a fisherman
than to a blacksmith, so worries seem greater to a person
who has not experienced them than to one who has.
Here in the crowd was a person who dismissed a wound
he received as something of little importance, yet thought
his reputation something great, and so I fell upon his
little story. I had seen Tullus Hostilius, the King, immediately. He thought he was someone unworthy, because he was a grandson of the Hostilius family. They
were well known for their defense of the Roman citadel
against the Sabines. In the midst of his rule he had been

killed by a bolt of lightning from the great Jupiter and was burned up with all his palace. He was spitting out unprintable oaths against Jupiter and the other gods.

I was laughing and would have listened to him at greater length if Tarquin the Elder, like the King before him a citizen of the same city, had not attracted my attention for a little while. When I finally put aside his complaint as well as that of Tullus Servius and the others who were there, Tarquin the Proud approached, and after I listened to his grieving more fully, I decided to describe it, for from his crime, that of his wife, and the unbelievable vice of his son, it can be shown that Roman liberty was born.

ABOUT TARQUIN THE PROUD,
HIS SON SEXTUS,
AND THE RAPE OF LUCRETIA

Tarquin would have been a great King except for his son's lust for his innocent relative.

Two sons were born to Tarquin the Elder, Aruns and Lucius, and at his death they were still young men. Previously, when Servius Tullus was still a child sleeping in his cradle, a flame came down from the sky and lit on his head, a happy sign for the future of the kingdom. So on the advice of Queen Tanaquil he succeeded to the throne on the death of the king, Tarquin the Elder, and when the young princes were old enough, he joined them to his daughters in marriage.

Just as the innate qualities of the young men were different, so were the characteristics of their wives. Aruns, by nature mild, had as his wife Tullia the

Younger, who was very fiery. In contrast Lucius, fierce by nature, by chance married the elder Tullia, who was very mild. Tullia the Younger, the fiery one, tolerated the humility of her husband and the quiet of her sister with great impatience. It happened that Aruns and the elder sister died, and because of their harmony, Lucius Tarquin and the surviving Tullia were married, Servius more quiet about it than approving.

Tullia, because of her impatient nature, continuously prodded her husband and aroused this impetuous young man to such an extent that he took an opportunity to enter the council chamber and sit down in the place reserved for the King. He called together the patriarchs of the city and issued laws. When Servius came into the chamber with his own followers, Tarquin ejected them by force, and as they were leaving, he had them slaughtered. Then he ruled by the order of the people and the patricians. When he had accomplished these things, his cruel wife could not restrain herself. First, in a chariot she entered the court and excitedly saluted her husband as King. Then, as she was going back, she saw her father ignobly slaughtered lying in the middle of the street. Her chariot driver was horrified at the monstrous sight and wanted to turn so the wheels of the chariot would not touch the dead body. Tullia forbade him, however, and with the feet of the horses and the wheels of the chariot they ran over the body she despised and went on their way.

It was in this disgraceful way that Tarquin seized the power of the kingdom. (Apparently, someone had released Misfortune from her stake, for the events that follow will not end differently from the way they began.) Before anything else, the new king moved against the city fathers and the people and easily acquired the name of Proud. Both within the city and without he accomplished many great things to increase his own renown and that of the Romans. At home he constructed several temples to the gods that had been promised by the former kings. And in the same way he built the huge Temple of Jupiter on the citadel, the public water system, and other magnificent projects.

But the more exalted a person is, the closer he is to ruin, and Fortune endures his elevation with displeasure. More than anything else Tarquin wished to subjugate Ardea, the ancient city of the Rutuli, and so laid siege to it. This business was drawn out for a long time, and some young men had gathered together in the camp of the king. After the food had been taken away they were drunk on the wine, and began to talk about the chastity of their wives. Each extolled his wife above the others. So their deeds might be tested, secretly they mounted their horses and each hurried to his house with his friends. They agreed to extol the one whom they would find engaged in the most praiseworthy occupation. They saw that the women in the court were given to playing, but at Collatia Lucretia was modestly passing the night with her servants spinning wool. She, they thought, was the most worthy of praise.

But for her virtue it happened that this chaste woman received a cruel reward. It was her simple beauty, aided by nothing more artificial than her uprightness, that enticed Sextus Tarquin, the son of Tarquin the Proud, to her. The young man was so aroused that he desired her with all his longing. After a few days Sextus was driven back to her by his inexpressible lust, and without anyone knowing it, the very chaste woman received him hospitably at Collatia, because he was a relative of her husband's. He was honored graciously and kindly for she had no suspicions whatsoever about him. While they ate, he observed sagaciously the routine of the house. But later, during a stormy night, he went into the room when Lucretia slept. By this adulterer's drawn sword she was threatened not with death but with disgrace, for he forced himself into her embrace against her wishes. After he had gratified his pleasure, he left.

Her mind was not able to bear the shameful invasion of her privacy. When morning came, she summoned all her servants and revealed to them what had taken place. With a sword she had hidden in her clothes, she propitiated her violated body with her death. The pure, innocent blood flowing from the deep wound brought death to the woman as it brought freedom to the state.

It was Junius Brutus who drew the sword from the wound and with Lucius and Collatinus revealed this unspeakable crime. And advocating liberty for the people, he took over power not only in Collatia but also in the city of Rome. When he was admitted into the camp of Tarquin the Proud he made the crime known there and proclaimed liberty for all. When Tarquin, enraged and threatening, returned to Rome, the city was closed against him; so he attacked Ardea, and while he did so, in Rome, he lost a son in death. The old proverb was reversed: when the son eats sour grapes, the parents feel it in their mouths.

Tarquin found his affairs in this state: deprived of his kingdom and without an army he was forced to seek exile with all his family. Where his nefarious Tullia went I do not remember reading. Sextus turned to the Gabii whom before he had deceived, and (it is very sure) was executed by them. Tarquin the Proud, however, still in exile, tried to regain his kingdom by subterfuge, but was not successful against the strength of the Romans. Aided by his friends the Etruscans, by Porsinna, the King of Clusium, then by the Latin people, he took to war. But the attack went badly; and Aruns, with another of his sons, and Octavius Mamilius, the leader of the Latins, surrendered with all his people. A miserable old man, Tarquin went to Cumae where he wasted away an unhappy old age as a private citizen under Aristomen, the tyrant of that city.

AGAINST THE PRODIGIOUS LUST OF PRINCES

Although some use history to defend their lusting, there is more evidence against it.

Even if I wished, I could not restrain my vehemence against those in high places. For the most part, they so hate chastity that if a whole multitude of women gathered together to fulfill their desires, the women could still not satisfy their lusts. These students of passions feast their eyes in churches, squares, public buildings— everywhere that elegant women assemble. Then, excited by their disreputable hunger, they arrange to fulfill their craving. They want all young women. Implementing their hopes with their power, they snare their prey with various lures: these with smooth talk; those with threats; others with gifts, a few with promises, and if nothing else suffices, some they drive into the nets of their delights by force. And vaunting their frenzy in song and dance, they think it is a very great achievement to have polluted someone's marriage bed. If anyone happens to speak against the zeal of their crimes, immediately they rise up shamelessly and explain their disgraces as if they had the most sanctified reasons.

"Think of David's adultery with Bethsabea, of Samson's with a prostitute, of Solomon's with the idolatrous

woman, and many other examples of the same kind."
They add that sexual freedom is above all the sport of
young men, a crime the result of our nature, not the
result of malice, and that they cannot bridle their youth.
They are forced into what they do and do not harm
anyone. In the maturity of their old age they will be
continent.

Oh, this awfully stupid group of men! Oh, the ridicu-
lousness of it! The fatuous hair-splitting! They cannot
deny that these holy men were punished for their crimes.
When David committed his sin, he wept, nor did his
tears cease until he knew he had mitigated God's wrath.
If Samson sinned with Delilah, then his blindness and
his long captivity should strike terror into these young
princes. Also Solomon, deprived of the Holy Ghost,
recognized his sin and desisted from it.

But these princes do not weep; they do not desist, nor
do they fear the judgment of God. If we are of a mind
to imitate the evil deeds of these holy men, should not
we rather imitate them when they accomplish something
worthwhile? They were lascivious and sinned, but also
they were valorous in war, they cultivated justice, were
remarkable for their bounty, were remembered by those
who obeyed them and remembered for obeying God.
Those who wish to be like them in their lewdness and
disdain the other side of their lives act like the hawk.
All day long he sails around with his wings extended and
sees many things he might choose to eat, but still he
always chooses something putrefying.

I do not deny that human nature inclines in this direction. The sin of lust should not arise out of the sport
of youth; it should be its scorn. The more inclined an
age is to passion, the more severely should curbs be
imposed. I wish those who exalt these men and excuse
their degradation would direct their eyes on Scipio, who

later was given the name Africanus. He brought his beautiful bride from her captivity at Luceium still chaste. Above all let them ponder Cato the Censor, who, surrounded by the delights of Cyprus, diligently kept himself free from all its infectious temptations. And these same princes should give their attention to Drusus, who kept all desires of the flesh within the limits of his marriage bed.

"What!" they will exclaim, "these people were not young. They did not have any virility left." But why do I call the most firm men to their attention to save their purity of body and soul, when we read how often tender young girls have held out only slightly against the dire threats of the tyrants? Wives were given to men to have children, and they suffice to satisfy any passionate inclinations. In addition, these princes say disgracefully and foolishly that what they do is their own affair as if each one were allowed to do what pleases him. However, it is reason that separates man with his customs from brutes, and so man has made laws. Whoever breaks them immediately turns himself from a man into a beast. Men should use their strength to protect womanly honor from violence. Yet what greater folly can a woman commit than to take someone to guard her welfare or to put herself and all her goods in the power of someone who has stained her grace and honor? I am harmed if my home is destroyed by an adulterer as if I, myself, were shamed.

It is readily apparent that lords are honored by the people because the lords protect them, not because they injure them. To no one is it permitted to be as free as he wishes if he acts against the public trust. If he does so, he acts in vain. If he objects, the people demand that he observe it. I ask, why do I need a king, if he takes away the honor of a woman whom without him

I might perhaps have saved? Observe what happens to these rulers who allow themselves to fall into license. They are able to take away riches and afterward to restore them; to occupy lands, then to leave them unharmed; to destroy houses, and to build them up again. The ruler can send someone into exile and call him back again, can deprive someone of public honors, then restore them. But chastity once violated can never be restored, nor can this stain ever be washed away. The Roman people were able to bear arms, to follow their king to his camp and on his command to go into battle. They shed their blood and gave up their lives. They worked in public sewers, on the foundations of great edifices; they expended their sweat and labor; they paid taxes and endured all the hardships of rule. But they were not able to endure the violation of Lucretia. On the contrary, they rose up and rebelled against their king and sent him from the kingdom into perpetual exile. Virginius, because of this same crime, was able to put the Decemvir Claudius into prison. From the violation of Dina resulted the destruction of the Sicimiti. Because of Helen, Troy fell, and the Tribe of Benjamin, because of the shameful union of Levita, was reduced almost to nothing. Holofernes of Assyria, while awaiting a victory in battle, suffered rightful punishment even before he committed his crime, and fell from a blow of his own sword, wielded by the woman whose embrace he desired so shamefully.

What do I urge by these examples? A man may walk the public highways but must leave alone the fields enclosed with hedges. If these lovers of base vice do not wish to leave danger alone, at least they should guard their health. Continuous lust dulls the mind, reduces the memory, saps the strength, and is the enemy of well-being. If licentiousness is continued into old age, many diseases result; so not only should chastity be guarded, but the lewdness of a misspent youth should also be deplored.

ABOUT XERXES,
KING OF THE PERSIANS

*The largest army ever assembled was defeated
by a combination of bravery, strategy, and
the forces of nature.*

I still had not said enough against lust when suddenly I was besieged by many rulers. It occurred to me that at the beginning of this work I suffered from a lack of stories, but now I was wearied by their abundance. Never before had I seen such a great throng of mourners. One of them, it seemed, was Marcius Coriolanus. He was recreant, driven into exile by the ingratitude of the Romans. He had listened to the prayers of his mother and for this was killed by the Volces. But I saw Xerxes coming toward me bemoaning his pride, and I sent away the others to take up his story.

Xerxes, the son of Darius, King of the Persians, and of the daughter of King Cyrus, succeeded his father to the throne after he had settled the disputes about the succession with his older brother Artemenes. He had such an abundance of riches, such regal brilliance, such a great number of subjects, that scarcely anyone the equal of him can be found at any time in history. His foolish mind was so puffed up by these things that he dared to believe he could conquer not only the world, but if he wished, could take heaven away from the gods. This swollen pride God did not endure for long.

Near the beginning of his reign, after Aristides had been ignominiously driven out, Xerxes occupied Egypt, which revolted against his father. Then he completed the preparations for war against the Greeks that Darius had begun not long before. It took five years. When he had gathered together seven hundred thousand soldiers from Persia, three hundred thousand from other places, an enormous fleet, and all kinds of engines of war as well, he left Persia, intending to occupy the country and sea of the Greeks. To have gathered so many people together in arms, however, was prodigious; for when they marched out not only did they cover everything, but also they cut away the mountains, filled up the valleys, and exhausted springs and rivers. Since he had not feared to conquer the land, he did not think the sea unworthy of his attention either. He spanned the expanse which others had only with difficulty crossed with ships. From Abydos to Sestos he built a bridge fantastic in size, and with his army he crossed over from Asia into Europe on foot. This had never been heard of before, nor has any imitator dared follow him.

But what must be, Fortune accomplished. Indeed, his crossing was neither so famous nor outstanding that his return was not more shameful and feeble. For the Lacedemonians were informed by the letters of Demaratus, their king, an exile with Xerxes, concerning the efforts of the Persians, so they could prevent his strategy. He advised them to send Leonidas, a celebrated military commander of his time, with a small band of armed men. There were no more of them than four thousand soldiers. With these troops this famous man, who did not know the meaning of despair, occupied the pass of Thermopylae. Here for three days they gave battle, resulting in a great and bloody slaughter of the Persians, and held them from advancing. However, Leonidas saw that the top of the mountain looming over the valley was occupied by eighty thousand of the enemy. When he had sent away his allies, there were only six hundred Spartans to die to save the state. He ordered them to breakfast as if they were likely to take supper in Hell. However, when it was night, with a fervor equal to all his army, they entered the camp of five hundred thousand Persian soldiers, and while they were asleep from wine, the Spartans sent them to their graves. Everything was in confusion; the slaughter did not stop until late the next day, but the Lacedemonians and their leader eventually fell, exhausted from the fast and the long killing. They were covered with blood, unconquered, and they had acquired eternal fame. In the tumult and confusion Xerxes fled, wounded and unknown. The anguish of the flight made him so thirsty that, with his own hands as a cup, he was forced to drink water stained with the blood that his solders had lost, and afterward he dared assert that never had he tasted a drink that was sweeter.

This was the first visitation that an angry Fortune made on him; but soon another visit came unexpectedly, that in relation to the preceding one might *seem* less, but was not less shameful to the proud king. As if he waged war not only against mankind but also against the gods, he sent four thousand soldiers to the temple of Apollo at Delphi to raze it. While Xerxes was waiting for news of this destruction, he heard instead that the soldiers had all perished miserably by the power of the wind and rains and the fire of lightning.

He saw that his war on land went badly but, still swollen with pride, he wanted to battle the strength of the sea with his navy. His fleet covered almost all the sea, and at Salamis he met the fleet of Athens under the leadership of Themistocles. Actually Xerxes was con-

quered more by military skill than by force of arms. At
the beginning of the battle, when the allies of Xerxes
approached with their ships, the Ionians (because of
whom the Athenians waged war) by Themistocles' order
began to turn the prows of their ships about. This
maneuver inspired and strengthened the Athenians, but
frightened the Persians. Xerxes watched. He was as
proud in his palace as he was fearful here. Artemisia,
Queen of Halicarnassus, came to his aid, and as if she
had changed sex with Xerxes fought very savagely among
the chief leaders of the battle so the Persians might not
be put to flight. In the battle the Athenians followed
after the king's fleet. Many of the king's ships were
seized and sunk, and a great destruction took place.

And in this way the king was struck three times by
misfortune, and was barred from his proud intent. As
he was about to go back into Persia Xerxes took the
advice of Mardonius and put him in charge of three
hundred thousand troops to destroy all of Greece, while
Xerxes returned by another way. But the skill of Themistocles tricked him. As he started to withdraw, he was
frightened and left his generals. With a few men he
fled to cross over by a bridge that he had made. He
discovered it had been toppled and destroyed by the
winter storms. As if the enemy were right behind him,
still shaking he entered into a small fishing boat, and
begged the seamen to take him to the opposite shore as
quickly as possible. When he had landed, he stood for
a long time alone on the shore, unaccompanied by even
a single servant boy.

Nor was this the last wound of Fortune. Almost all
those whom he had abandoned when they hurriedly fled
had been driven off the roads and killed by exertion,
hunger, thirst, or disease, so that there was no hill, road,
or field which was not covered far and wide with the

bodies of dead Persians. Xerxes arrived at his home with very few soldiers. Not long afterward he received the sad news that Mardonius' whole army had been destroyed in a single battle in Boeotia. The camp had been captured, and all his royal wealth had been divided up among the Greeks. With a few others Mardonius had been saved, but something almost unbelievable happened to his army. On the same day that the troops of Mardonius fell, the Persians fought in Asia at Mycale; around the middle of the day, before the fight started (the fleets visible to each other), the news reached both sides that Mardonius had fled and his army was destroyed. As the Greek strength increased, the Persian diminished. As soon as the signal for the battle was given, there was a great slaughter of Persians, who turned and fled. Thus the news of the first and the second disaster reached the king in rapid succession.

But these injuries and disgraces were not sufficient for the king, who decided to tempt Fortune once again. After he had reorganized his forces, he gave battle both on land and on the sea, with the same result as before. The entire Persian army, under the leadership of Cimon, the son of Miltiades, was destroyed at the river Eurimedonte. These disasters caused Xerxes to be hated and despised by the Persians. With the reputation of the king weakened, Artabanus, one of his prefects, with seven of his strongest sons, entered the palace one evening in the hope of taking over the kingdom. They slaughtered the unwary king, and so the monarch's extravagant pride passed away with his life's blood.

THE DARK BLINDNESS OF MANKIND

*Why are we always duped by outward appearances,
and why do we always search after trifles?*

What misery is this? What blindness? What crime? If
the earth is shaken a little, we immediately leave the
cities and flee into the country. If a wild animal breaks
out of his cage, immediately we bar our doors. If a
river overflows, we climb its banks to higher ground.
We call a doctor so we may save the oppressive life of
the body a little longer. But we run after a bauble that
is certain to ruin us and will frequently destroy our body
and soul. Alas, I have said to myself, how foolish we
are to run after it. Even when this desire is not at hand
we seek it ardently through heat and cold, through
mountains, plains, and the sea; through a thousand
mortal hazards, through crimes and violence, with
nervous exertion and insuperable labor. When our lives
are devoid of such experiences, we proclaim we are
truly miserable.

We do not care for the sky, remarkable for its clear
serenity, the brilliant sun, the silvery moon, the glittering
stars, and the other permanent beauties of the heavens
circling around us in continual motion. God, calling us
to the true glory with paternal affection, promising us
His eternal kingdom, His unfailing truth following His
judgment, all this we despise as a lie. I do not know
by what madness it is that with deadly seriousness we
fix our eyes on the ground, stop up our ears, harden our
heart, and while we do not see what cares worldly glitter
may hide, what poisons it may bear, and what chances
it may be subject to, we think only of all the delights

that have fallen to us and forget what God has taught us. Worse, we see that glitter droops, falls, is reduced to nothing; but still, to our misfortune, we imagine it to be fixed and everlasting.

Oh, miserable creatures that we are, let us put aside this insatiable desire by which the eyes of our soul are blinded. Let our belief give way to reason. Although we are weary of regarding the Heavens and listening to God, at least every day we should be intent upon those things that are come right in front of our eyes. And so that heaps of treasure, numerous acquaintances, or the splendor of honors may not deceive us, among the many who emerged from that recent group, let us study Xerxes. That king, who left Persia with the greatest pomp and fully armed, who had the greatest hope in himself and his plans, returned to his country unarmed, obscure instead of triumphant, and received the mourning of his people. He who commanded the downfall of the gods (whatever was trivial, he regarded highly) was slaughtered in his own palace by Artabanus.

Why should we say more? What more can we ask in order to see what riches, power, and a temporal kingdom can do? What do we strive after, search for, hope for, or even know? I ignore the hidden cares by which all outward show is infected, and invoke the outward appearance only. Would it not have been better for Xerxes to be deprived of those outward things? And is it not one of the greatest misfortunes that he was happy? Why do we not drive this cloud of ignorance away from our eyes? But we, miserable creatures, turn aside. God may have many a Themistocles and Leonidas, but we have even a larger army than Xerxes. Yet finally deprived of our temporal abundance, in flight and powerless, we in vain beg the inexorable boatmen, not at the Hellespont, but on Acheron's shore; and naked, alone, and mournful, we cry exhausted, having lost the hope of a better life.

SOME UNHAPPY PEOPLE

The author wished to rest, but the
mournful people continued to arrive.

Having inveighed against our folly, I sat down, for a little time, to get my breath. But not for long. When I sat down, I was surrounded by people lamenting their lot. While I gave them my attention, I realized that not only Asia had experienced ruin. Not against kings alone were the arrows of Fortune thrown, but actually whoever rose up, had always fallen, and the depth of their fall was in proportion to the height to which they had risen. I could have demonstrated this at some length with the Italians, but was now called back (although unwillingly) to write of some private downfalls, because Artabanus, Xerxes' murderer, complained with a great flow of tears that after a promising start he had a pitiful finish. In the midst of all this, I met Phalanthus, a very ancient leader of the Spartans, complaining that he had been exiled to Brundusium by his own Tarentinians. I was drawn along with him where I was summoned, and as I arrived I saw Caeso Quintius, who asserted that he had been unjustly condemned to exile. Immediately after I sent him away, I heard Cloelius Graccus, leader of the cavalry, cursing the gods and Fortune. Conquered by Cincinnatus, he, as a captive, went before his chariot in a triumphal march. Then I saw Appius Claudius, the decemvir. His head was covered with a veil, his garments filthy, and he passed me silently, in the hope that I would not recognize him. But I selected his unhappy story because from an originator of laws he developed into a servant of license and a proud man. I decided to write about his disgrace and about others like him.

ABOUT APPIUS CLAUDIUS, THE DECEMVIR

A learned judge let his infatuation for Virginia disrupt court procedure and so brought on a revolution.

It was discovered that the Claudian family went to Rome after being driven out of the Sabine city of Regillus by its rulers, because of a rebellion of the citizens lead by Appius Clausius, afterward called Appius Claudius. The family was received among the Patricians, and many Appians were born from the family, almost all the line of men exceedingly hostile to the Plebians.

When the ambassadors returned from Athens with Attic laws, it happened that the consuls were deposed. Ten men were chosen at Rome who drafted these laws as the convenience of the Romans demanded, and with everyone's consent they executed them. Very great power was granted these men, and there was no appeal against them. One of the Claudian family, Appius Claudius, was made a decemvir. With his colleagues he ruled temperately and wrote laws according to the demands of the time, so it seemed to the citizens that, when his year had passed, he should be elected to the office for the following year. Now Appius, a man of great spirit, was delighted by such prominence and sought it with great eagerness. He conducted himself so that the fathers of the city easily perceived what was on his mind: that by the succession, the great power would seem to be perpetuated in him. So that he would not obtain this, they tried (in vain) to oppose his culpable ambition. With the consent of the senate Appius was ordered to call an assembly to elect the future decemvirs, and to say who, in his judgment, was suitable to the republic.

These distinguished men thought that, when they had granted him this liberty, shame would prevent him from naming himself one of the decemvirs. But what does the unbridled desire for power not dare? Appius, having put aside all honor, contrary to everyone's expectation designated himself one of the decemvirs for the future year before anyone else. This would have been monstrous even among those who conducted themselves with raging wickedness, but even more so among citizens still living with an elementary sagacity and moderation. Truly, it seemed to this ambitious man that he had not done enough. The lictors who preceded them were accustomed to bear the *fasces*, symbols of power, in turn. Appius, however, established that they carry them not in turn, but each one continuously. And so in place of twelve lictors a hundred and twenty with battle-axes and *fasces* were seen going before Appius in the Palace of Justice and the Forum, arousing fear in both the people and the senate. Appius, emboldened by his own malice as well as by the patience of the citizens, was so haughty that he appeared not as a decemvir or public official, but rather as a king with his followers. Then he began to act on his own to punish some, to allow others to go unpunished; to raise these up, and to push others down.

When affairs were in this state, at Algidum [1] a war broke out against the Volces and the Equi, and the rest of the decemvirs left the province in order to lead

---

[1] Modern Pava, in the mountains southeast of Rome.

the army. At that time this evil man descended from the
pinnacle that he had achieved by fraud. Either by the
wish of the Roman Fortune or by the impetus of his
own iniquity, he allowed his roving eye to be caught
by an attractive young girl whose name was Virginia. He
became completely entranced by her beauty and finally
burned with an overwhelming passion. Although both
his flattery and his gifts were rejected by the young
girl, still he thought it was not safe to use force obviously. She was the daughter of Lucius Virginius, a
Plebian, but one well known and just, honorable, and
magnanimous for his rank. Also Virginia was affianced to
Lucius Icilius, a tribune of the Plebians and a very brave
young man. Appius therefore turned to a gigantic deceit
to satisfy his desires. He subborned Marcus Claudius,
his client, to say that the girl was his slave, and a few
days later, when she was passing in the Forum, Claudius
seized her. When she resisted forcibly, he personally
dragged her away.

At the court of Appius the girl wept and invoked the
honor of her fiance. Publius Numitorius, the girl's uncle,
and Lucius Icilius, her fiance, arrived; and after a great
deal of disagreement they obtained a deferment of judgment until the next day when Virginia's father was
called from the military camp. Opportunely — except
for the hopes of Claudius — Virginius (still disarrayed
from the camp) entered the court with his daughter. He
spoke out, and so they would not desert him he pleaded
fervently with those who were standing there, not only
for himself and his daughter, but also at length for freedom in general. Icilius and Numitorius did the same to
the crowds of friends and relations who had pressed
around. Then leaving the citizens that surrounded him
on all sides, Appius ascended the tribunal. Without listening to Virginius he said a few words for the plaintiff,

then pronounced a judgment from his filthy mouth proclaiming Virginia the slave of Claudius. Oh, what a famous judge! What an outstanding law-giver! Actually I ask whether in this very brilliant judgment, the mind of Aeacus [2] was not resurrected from the center of Hell.

All present were astounded when they heard this. Virginius was aroused and spoke forcefully but in vain. When Claudius wished to take away what had been adjudged to him, on the order of Appius, the milling crowd gave way. Virginius requested the small favor of speaking with his daughter and her nurse, and, as if to talk with them, took them toward the shop of Cloacina. He picked up one of the butchering knives from the rack that was there, and weeping, said, "In the only way that I can, I save your freedom." And when he had thrust the knife into her breast, he continued, "Let me say, I prefer to be the savage killer of a virgin rather than the indulgent father of a whore." And to Appius, who was watching the deed with a wild countenance, he said, "On you and your head I call down this sacred blood." Then, when he had drawn the knife, dripping with blood, out of his daughter's maidenly breast, he made a passage for himself amongst the soldiers there, and with his many friends left the city. Meanwhile there was a great uproar around the dead Virginia. The women howled, and Icilius and Numitorius shouted and raised up the inanimate body. To the noisy crowd they showed her pallid face, her mournful beauty, and her limbs, drooping in death. They pleaded her cause, and made the evil grow with their words.

Virginius came to Algidum, and Icilius fled to the land of the Sabines. He escaped the hands of the lictors with their help, and, like Virginius in Algidum, made known

[2] The grandfather of Achilles who, because of his just government, was made one of the three judges of the underworld.

Appius' lust, his violence, his shameful judgment, and all that followed. A military rebellion immediately took place. The soldiers left their camp, and after they joined up with the army, they came into the Aventine Hill and from there to the Sacred Mount, as if they advanced the destiny of Plebian liberty. All the people who remained in the city ran to them, and the city seemed deserted. They would not be reconciled with the Senate until the Senate took away the power of the decemvirs, until they created a tribune of the Plebians, and until they reinstated all the laws that the decemvirs had taken away.

So Appius, with all the other decemvirs, was toppled from his high position. Now a private citizen, he was apprehensive and feared those whom before he had arrogantly terrorized. On the very day that he had abdicated his power as a decemvir and the power of the tribune of the people had been confirmed, he was called by Virginius, now a tribune. Coming before the tribunal of his neighbors, Appius would plead his case. Where once he had held the highest place, he now occupied the lowest. He remembered that when he was a judge, he had been reproached by Virginius, then a private citizen, for his license and tyranny. Appius had seen him, putting aside his duty as a parent, repudiate and avenge with his knife the judgment against his daughter. Now Virginius would have his hard revenge against him, a private citizen himself, for the daughter and her honor. Nor was he wrong, for neither the crowd of young noblemen around him, nor his frequent appeals to the people, nor the prayers of his old uncle could mitigate the severity of the tribunal and of Virginius' judgment.

He who had unjustly refused to hear Virginius was now lawfully bound in chains by the court officials, and in the greatest shame taken to prison, to remain there until the day came for his defense. Until that day came this very base and tricky law-giver remembered the glory of his eminence, and the fame of his ancestors. He felt himself abandoned by his men and enveloped in disgraceful ignominy, not the worst, condemned by a Plebian, to the acclaim of the Plebians. At last his pride and anger turned into madness, and he brought death to himself among the filth and chains of the prison. And so, in order to appease the spirit of the innocent Virginia with an equivalent sacrifice, Spurius was killed—an associate of the criminal, a decemvir who had been unrelenting against her. The rest of the ten, with Marcus Clauius the special plaintiff, were sent into exile, and the personal property of both Appius and Spurius was restored to the public by the tribune of the Plebians.

Oh, you too happy freedom of the Romans, you would have endured forever, if every time that your rulers indulged themselves in licentiousness you remembered that you were twice redeemed by the blood of a chaste woman, and, sharp avengress, you appeared. But why? We mortals cannot remedy what has been destroyed by God's judgment.

AGAINST IGNORANT LAWYERS

The practice of the law can be no better than the training of its lawyers and judges.

Many things followed from the censure of Appius; but the enormous number of vices of the lawyers of today calls for an attack of the most righteous indignation against them. The ancients designated the most distinguished men and those versed in the sacred teachings of philosophy to take up the practice of law. They were selected not only for their complete knowledge of the law, but also for their maturity of conduct, their sanctity of character, and their venerable age. Besides Phoroneus, Minos, Lycurgus, Solomon, and others most ancient and foreign born, the Romans had such judges as Sempronius, Cato the Censor, Lucius Crassus, and Servius Sulpicius after the corrupt Appius. The present time, on the other hand, despises the skill of the ancients. Young children are not only taken away from the rules of grammar, but also from the rod of their nurses. They are placed not in schools but in brothels, where the most sacred laws of learning are violated by disgraceful adultery.

This is not done, as some try to allege, in order that the young person, who will not lose what was strongly impressed on the mind, be trained in the law, but in order that very early he be given over to avarice. Nor do they fear to profess this openly with resounding clamor, those who mount the academic chairs and rostra in their fur-trimmed robes. Proofs based on philosophy they ignore as if it were something redundant, and it is on these that justice is built and the customs of mankind are improved. From a swinish mouth they spew out an obscene vocabulary.

But let us put these scandals aside. They are superfluous, for they do not teach us how these lawyers conduct themselves to earn their bread. They are like jackasses in robes. The problems they do not understand, they ignore. Shamefully they try, if they can, to corrupt the law, and they apply all their efforts to deprive it of its simplicity and sanctity so that they can spread an unwelcome discord among the people. The wrangling of their litigants they stretch out eternally by their caviling.

And they loudly proclaim their pride in deceiving ever-lasting truth through clever trickeries and abominations. Anyone who through fraud becomes wealthy, they proclaim a father of the law and a pillar of the court. They revere him as a high priest of truth, archive of jurisprudence.

Oh, unyielding judgment of God; how long will You suffer these things? From such schools (in which I do not know whether they teach the surest way to seek the truth or to win bread) have repeatedly come counselors, judges, and advocates, with hands tainted, eyes wandering, license unrestrained, heart stony, sincerity a pretense, tongue honeyed, teeth like iron, and, in short, with an insatiable passion for gold. On that account, oh republic of Italy, you, who almost alone are observant of the laws of the Caesars, live in joy protected by advocates holy and outstanding, saved by just guards, enlightened by brilliant teachers! Go and form marriages secure from adultery, protect your young girls from ravishment and your religious from incest! Collect gold, cultivate fields, build houses as you wish, fashion laws for the future, and whatever you want turn to your benefit! But in the meantime the courts are occupied with avarice and license, and their counsels are lies and deceits. The ancient Romans rid themselves of Appius, but you, with your blindness to virtue, have raised up another who endures forever.

ABOUT ALCIBIADES,
THE ATHENIAN

The exiled King returned to Athens a hero, though eventually he was defeated and died in ill repute.

I will not deny that I was aroused against the villainous abuse of men who at this time have shamelessly usurped the title of lawgivers. Except that a few with reverence for the law are opposed. These are the ones by whose courage complicated laws are revealed; they are examples of the integrity of our forefathers. Because of these men my anger abated, and I turned my attention to those who were approaching, clamoring mournfully. Among them was Alcibiades, who no less than any had suffered the blows of our stepmother, Fortune. As I was relating the misfortunes of those in foreign countries rather than our own, I decided to add him to those I had described before.

Let me cover his manifold gifts in a few words. Alcibiades, from the city-state of Athens, was in his ancestry exceptional, in his body handsome, in warfare expert, in eloquence admired, and possessed such ability that he could easily turn himself to whatever skills he wished. From his youth he showed what kind of a leader of his city he would turn out to be. His uncle, Pericles, within his palace, was anxiously thinking how to render an accounting of public funds for the expense in building the gateway of Minerva; Alcibiades said to him, "Search to find a way not to give the accounting." Admiring the advice of the child, Pericles easily found such a way.

When his youth had come to the full flower of maturity, his appearance and habits promised great things. With the general consent of all the Athenians he was made a third leader of the fleet against Syracuse under Nicias and Lamachus. But either by the strength of Fortune or by the fault of the leaders, he had less success with military affairs. He was accused of various things by the governors of the republic, and, not without very great dishonor, was recalled. From a great leader he became a private citizen. Realizing that the favor of the citizens had changed, and agitated by the dishonor that had befallen him, he silently and voluntarily went into exile in Elis. Then he learned that the fury of the Athenians was aroused against him, and that the college of priests had publicly consecrated his head as as a sacrifice to the gods. His anger turned into hate, and he took himself to Sparta. Here he was better accepted because of a naval battle badly fought by the leaders of Athens in Sicily, where the Athenians were beaten and almost destroyed. Alcibiades persuaded Agis, King of the Lacedemonians, against the destruction of the Athenians. So that foreign groups would not take vengeance upon him, with a fleet assembled in Lacedemonia, he went not as a mercenary soldier but as a leader, albeit he was a private citizen. He rode into Asia, and the fame of his name was such that he easily drew many cities, tributaries, and allies of Athens from this alliance into one with Lacedemonia. This was a tremendous feat for any leader, not to speak of an exile from Athens. Finally he accomplished many outstanding deeds in the pursuit of the war, and had the opportunity to acquire great glory for himself; but because he acquired too much rather than too little, he aroused great envy among the leaders of the Spartans.

The light of his valor would have overcome the darkness of his exile, if the bitterness of secret envy had not attached itself equally to his widespread reputation. For when the leaders of the Lacedemonians thought that the tremendous glory of Alcibiades' name obscured theirs, not daring anything openly, they set traps secretly for him; nor would he have escaped this misfortune, except that help appeared that actually should have harmed him. He was intimate with the wife of King Agis, for his handsomeness had resulted in an affair with her. She had a premonition about these traps and in her sympathy toward her lover revealed what was contrived against him. Alcibiades was frightened by what she told him, and, on her advice, fled.

His mind changed against these enemies who deserved animosity, and he now became loyal to his own country. He joined Tissaphernes, with whom Darius the Persian, allied with the people of Sparta, planned total war against the Athenians. The eloquence of Alcibiades easily captivated their complete friendship and proved to them that they should not give aid to the Lacedemonians. When they were convinced, he got back the greatest part of the help they had earlier sent out. Then secretly making known to his fellow citizens all that the Persians did, he demonstrated that, although an exile, he was still fulfilling his duty to them. When he had calmed some of the hatred of the citizens against him, he promised them the friendship of Darius if they would transfer civil power from the people to the senate. That was afterwards accomplished, and what this astute man thought, immediately occurred; that is, because of the arrogant rule of the nobility, the people rebelled. To settle the rebellion, not only was Alcibiades recalled from his exile, but also, with the complete consent of the people, he was made leader both in civil and military affairs. Because of this spontaneous favor from the people, he boastfully promised the downfall of the nobility.

Moreover, the senate feared the power of a leader so cunning and energetic, and after trying in vain to turn the city over to the Lacedemonians, went into exile. Alcibiades had now accomplished what he wished; and when he had assuaged the civil ferment he prepared a huge fleet, and with great vigor began a battle against the Spartan leaders, Restromidarus and Pharnabazus. In this he was not only victorious, but when the leaders were killed, he captured or destroyed almost the entire fleet. Then Fortune tempted the Lacedemonians to a battle on the land, and here Alcibiades immediately transferred his victorious fleet into Asia, and devastated all the Lacedemonians there. He recalled to their old alliance all the cities who had defected from the Athenian confederation. He seized many others, and the efforts, of this one man, his many victories and transactions, restored the republic of Athens, perhaps about to perish. Then Alcibiades returned to Athens, where he had been greatly missed by his fellow-citizens, and was now greatly honored for his many successes. A multitude of citizens of all ages and both sexes eagerly went to meet him. Gratefully they carried their gods with them, these same people who, cursing, had offered Alcibiades' head to these gods.

They all admired him, and joyfully saluted him. All paid obeisance to him. They excused his former evil deeds, and now praised him to the sky, and promised voluntarily to link their fortunes with his, for with such a leader, they declared, Athens would be happy. They gave him honors more divine than human, and if they had been able, would have raised him up to Heaven. And so, he who had been condemned and had left Athens in secret, returned in pomp. On the very summit of glory, he did not remember that he had moved up and down, now joyous, now sad. He thought that because of his many victories and the present favor of the citizens, Fortune had laid a stable foundation under him.

But a huge change, more like an upheaval, was imminent. For when he heard that Cyrus had taken the place of Darius, the father, Alcibiades was about to release Misfortune from his stake. With too much confidence in Fortune he prepared the old fleet, and went over into Asia. Unopposed, he entered the lands, fertile from their long peace. The soldiers, wandering about, were suddenly surrounded, ambuscaded, and slaughtered. With no help available, the massacre was such that almost the whole power of the Athenians was brought to an end. This defeat changed the minds of the Athenians toward Alcibiades, who now awakened hatred in them. Conon was put in his place.

And so the height that Alcibiades had obtained with great resolution and effort was altered by a single adverse event, and from a prince he again became an exile. These many adverse circumstances drained the strength of the Athenians; and at the order of Lysander, leader of the Spartans, thirty of the most worthy surviving Athenians were selected to rule the republic. These rulers, fearing the cunning of the exile Alcibiades, developed into tyrants. When they discovered that he had gone to Artaxerxes, King of the Persians, they ordered that the road be patrolled, in order to intercept and to kill him.

Warned, Alcibiades could not easily be taken. But it happened, by the consent of a vengeful Fortune, that he was toppled from his high station, for he was burned alive while sleeping in his bedroom. His body was drawn from the fire consumed, and lay unburied. Not long before, as through in a dream, he had seen himself lying without a grave, covered with his mistress' dress.

This was the way Alcibiades experienced Fortune;

now happy, now sad, and almost as if in jest, he was now driven from his home, now recalled, then over-thrown once more. So this man, who in his youth had had a brilliant start, splendorous with great honors, in his old age was anxious and marked by exile, at finally suffered an obscure and chaotic death.

IN DEFENSE OF ALCIBIADES

The sin of a great man is to be driven by a stronger spirit than his strength allows.

Perhaps there are those who say (and up to this point they could say it very often) that Alcibiades brought these circumvolutions on himself. This I confess, but it does not matter to me, for anyone who wishes can become unhappy. This I have acknowledged, and truly I am glad to excuse this most prominent man and others like him in a few words. Rarely do I discover anyone content with his lot. This does not seem extraor-dinary. Our soul is implanted with a divine gift com-prising a fiery strength, a divine beginning, and an insatiable desire for glory. When the soul is a great one, not weakened by bodily sloth, it cannot be restrained in the little prison of the breast. It goes out, and its magnitude fills the entire world. Easily it transcends the stars, and, driven by fire, it burns with this sublime de-sire. Spurred by hope for the great things, as well as by eloquence, the soul regards laziness with horror; by whatever strength it has, it tries to drag along the mass of the body to which it was fastened at birth. But sometimes, deceived, the soul then goes in the opposite direction; though itself light, it is dragged downwards by the weight of the body. Examples of this are provided by those who complain in this little collection.

Therefore the vice of the noble spirit is this, that it wishes to ascend to higher things by another way than reason allows, but from where it usually falls. Everyone is thus misled many times, and if not on the path of wrong reason, then at least many times with a force greater than his strength allows. Thus, Alcibiades was filled with his own noble spirit, and in addition was driven by the noble deeds of his ancestors. He thought that Fortune would be milder to him than to the others. Magnanimous souls are frequently overthrown because the circumstances were the opposite of what they had hoped for.

Anyone longing for his own hearth, for domestic pleasure, could find no peace in civil honors or in high office. How could he find repose among the thousand troubles of exile, wishing to rid himself of disgrace, desirous of vengeance, burning to win his country back and receive again his country's honors? Although these continuous incentives did not drive the man, yet on the other hand he did not languish under the feet of Fortune in sloth. But no one, unless he were torpid and dull, would prefer to live in idleness and calm in preference to fighting the continual tempest of the ocean waves. If he had no other choice, he would rather be beaten incessantly by rocks than to lie among feathers in a perpetual sleep like Sardanapalus. For sloth extinguishes both strength of mind and body. In ferment, the mind is strengthened, and at the same time the power of the body is aroused. Sloth, with a kind of rust, dulls anything that was once bright. Activity brightens anything that was dull. It is well known that Ulysses, driven by the seas to leisurely Egypt, remained under the skies of this country. We condemn his willful inactivity, but we praise and admire his wanderings.

And so Alcibiades, though overthrown by many different causes, brought an extraordinary brilliance to his name that has lasted until our times. There were many names in his own time which were not less known than his and had no less chance for accomplishment; yet their name perished with their body, for these people dawdled in lethargy. It is therefore necessary to accomplish something, but for what you would do, you must look prudently. For us the road to Heaven is clear, but it was not to Alcibiades. We must sweat at everything we undertake; in that way we are not tranquilized into stagnation, and when we die suffer eternal torment.

THE AUTHOR ACQUITTED AND POETRY COMMENDED

How the life of a poet differs from most professions, and what its unique difficulties are.

I am afraid that while trying to guard against something, I get into trouble myself. Who doubts but that whatever someone is talking about, actually happens? Or that you commend laziness even as you are about to inveigh against it? I have an answer to that without any difficulty. While there is one kind of person, there are still many kinds of interests, and each person decides where he can achieve his own happiness as he wishes. For this reason a soldier chooses the wars, the lawyer the court, the farmer the fields—the examples can be infinite. The poet seeks out a solitary place and lives there. The soldier enjoys the tumult of battle, the lawyer enjoys argumentation and litigation, the farmer the beauty and greenery of the fields, the poet the harmonious sound of verses. The first is accustomed to combat, the second to judgments, the third to the progress of the seasons, and the last to contemplation. To the soldier the final goal is victory, to the lawyer it is money, to the farmer it is harvest, and to the poet it is reputation. This arises from a great complexity of professions, though each has only one end. What pleases one person is justifiably unattractive to another.

It is certainly not remarkable that when we consider these goals separately, each person desires one worthy of praise. In the case of Alcibiades, I praised his vigor and strength of arms but condemned sloth and torpor. Yet I did not condemn my own desire for repose. His goal was to make war, mine to write; and because of this, what he had to seek, I had to avoid if I were to achieve the end of a happy life. Actually I do not want people to think that poets seek out mountainous caves, shady forests, clear fountains, murmuring streams, as well as the joyful and withdrawn silence of the country, which the ancients and I have called restful, especially so they can better fill their stomachs and satisfy their passions. This is not true. The divine poet Homer and our Virgil, with his Heavenly inspiration would never have been able to increase their understanding of various celestial matters, even with their exalted intelligence, in the turbulent society of men or in the clatter and swirl of the city. They would never have seized those truths from the breast of Jupiter, as it were, nor gloriously revealed them to the present and to the future by the wonderful skill of their exquisite poems. Therefore these places have been called places of repose which were removed from all the noise of people. Often I have praised such places, and I desire them very much when they are available to me.

But I am not yet acquitted of blame. I am now harassed by a sharper attack. Some person might say, in how few words and how skillfully he wishes to make himself out a poet or to be believed a poet; to this end he affects the leisure of a poet. I confess that these are not the things that make me a poet, and I hold that a poet does not engage in such foolishness. I am bold enough to confess what I am, nor do I wish to be held what I am not. However, I wish to be and take great pains that I may be a poet. Whether I will arrive at the summit only God knows. I think that I do not have sufficient strength for so long a climb when along the way many passes, and cliffs almost insurmountable intervene. However, many ignorant persons have the opinion that the summit of poetry can be reached very easily. Although they do not have any idea what poetry is, with sour faces they claim that poets are liars, are men addicted to the use of fables, and like entertainers who make use of knowledge not their own. These people are the liars if they really believe what they say.

In reality poetry is a celebrated body of knowledge, elevated and beautiful, requiring skill. Only by the aid of poetry is it possible, within the limits of human weakness, to follow in the footsteps of Holy Writ. For as scripture reveals the secrets of the Divine Spirit and the prophecies of things to come under the guise of figures of speech, so poetry tries to relate its lofty concepts under the veils of fictions. If the highest type of man is a poet, then his poetry is the highest achievement. The ancients were not mistaken in their custom to give a crown of laurel only to those who had a triumphal

military reception, and to poets as a reward for their
work, and in testimony of their eternal powers. They
would not honor victors and liars with the same reward.

What we proposed we have now proved. If I wish
leisure, I do not wish it in order to be thought a poet,
but believing that leisure can confer many gifts on me
which for a time were sought by poets with the greatest
diligence. While dogs bay, the bright moon regularly
follows its course through the limpid expanse of the
night.

AGAINST RICHES,
THE FRENZY OF MANY

*Wealth brings worry and care, but satisfaction
with little brings freedom and joy.*

Nature has hidden gold in the most secret depths of
the earth, as it is dangerous to the human species. But
Avarice, the prospector, searches voraciously and brings
it to light. Avarice taught us to dig out the mountains,
tunnel the bowels of the earth, and even to invade the
depths of the sea with fish hooks. First, Avarice leveled
the height of the mountains and cut down the woods to
make roads. Then he showed us how to occupy foreign
shores, to sign false contracts, to deceive wild beasts,
to put serpents to sleep, to spread discord, to lie. He
armed mankind in violence, invented poisons and treach-
eries. By all these methods and others as well, he
gathered this glittering peril for some men in vast
quantities.

But even the most careful observer does not see what
enormous misfortunes the possessor of these vast quan-

tities acquires. He is gnawed by ulcerous care lest his wealth be infested by worms, consumed by fire, filched by thieves, seized by the state or by rebels. He is sleepless by night in order to hang on to it, and he even fears the scurrying of mice. He excites great envy, is tricked, and in both the flattery and hate of his children he knows that they watch for his death with anticipation.

Poverty is by far more tolerable than wealth, for unless a man has a strong will, he cannot endure wealth. The most ordinary servant girl is poor and happy. It is true that the ignorant and uninformed think there is no virtue in poverty. They admire the grand palace, robes glittering with gold, tables mountainous with food and drink, myriads of servants, and all those other things that, while they do not make a person distinguished, yet—in their judgment—make him seem rich.

The ignorant person does not realize that while the whole world resounded with the crash of war, Amiclate, free from care, was sleeping in his tent and Pompey was trembling with fear in his tall fortress at Dyrrhachium. Diogenes in his tub was tranquilly contemplating things celestial, while Sardanapalus inside his golden castle sought to hide away. Aglaus Psophidius was singing in the meadow while Zamaria perished in the conflagration of his palace. What other examples do we need? This is abundantly clear: people long for the heights, but there they are continually buffeted by lightning, the fury of the winds, the shock of the quake. But the lowly resist catastrophe. Few realize what vexations, tortures, and anxieties are hidden under luxurious garments. Many times these are not garments, but winding sheets decorated with gold and jewels for fetid cadavers.

Oh, I would rather be Atilius Regulus guiding the

plow with his hand, or Cincinnatus in his modest field turning over the clods of earth, both dressed for the farm, than I would be one of these rich and sinful worriers garbed in purple robes, dressed more for their own ostentation than for their own worth.

Nature is contented with little things. I will not press the point that early man lived on acorns and water, but will discuss those rulers who pampered themselves with delights. When Masinissa hid from Syphax in the caves of woods and mountains, was he not nourished by the roots or greenery that a few of his soldiers brought him? And Xerxes, richer than any other king, did he not quench his thirst, not with pure water, but on mud mixed with the blood of his soldiers? If this rough fare sustained the lives of kings, why do you need feasts to satisfy you? Perhaps a glutton would tell, but circumstances prevent him. I can tell you, though. Although these kings could do many things, still they had not yet achieved poverty as a virtue. Xerxes drank water from the hollow of his hands; after he had thrown his cup away, Diogenes did the same. Why do we, therefore, breathlessly search after superfluities? Poison is offered in gold and gems, but the brook runs clear of any dirt. But let us leave this, which perhaps seems farfetched.

In the country people are used to cooking food moderately rather than elaborately, and we observe that they, with their firm skin, endure the sun and the wind; they are content with plain clothes. Their strong and sinewy bodies shake down acorns from the oaks. They turn over the earth, sweat with never-ending labor, and are hardly ever weighed down with illness. Even in their old age they enjoy great vitality, as if they were still young. Do you think those who spend their time at great banquets and drinking are happy? Far from it. They are weak and soft from their indolence. After suffering from various and continual diseases, they bury their enfeebled youth in a premature grave. They are only eager for lots of servants because they cannot serve themselves.

But why do I weary myself in preaching so long? Wealth is glittering and in the eyes of fools seems very attractive. They do not want to recognize that the wealthy are agitated, hemmed in, miserable, and melancholy. We now leave this subject, but we shall return to it.

INTRODUCTION

I think that to some extent I have moved governors from their obstinacy and by the great examples of those who were elevated in spirit, I have frightened their insolence. For what man is so made of stone that he has been able to read how Priam fell though supported with so much strength; how Tarquin of Rome was driven into a miserable old age; how Xerxes, the Persian, though he invaded Greece with so great an army, fled alone to the shores of Asia. So if we can hope for the welfare of these governors, we are happy not to have labored in vain.

But it is not enough to have awakened those who were asleep, unless they have also been led into the clear light. They must develop strength of belief; then we will have fulfilled our promise that through the stories of our overthrown ancestors, their faith has increased.

ABOUT MARCUS MANLIUS CAPITOLINUS

*Though Manlius saved Rome from the Gauls,
his service was later forgotten.*

A great multitude of harassed and tearful Italians called out to me. The tremendous crowd carried on so, that I selected those whom I wanted and let the others pass on without notice. The man I chose was Marcus Manlius Capitolinus. He was a victim of envy, the result of his becoming chief magistrate of Rome. After achieving the highest place granted by Fortune, he ended his life shamefully and undeservedly in the turbid water of the Tiber.

The family of which Manlius was a member had exceptional splendor among the Romans and had been honored with the dignity of many noble titles. Marcus Manlius, surpassing his forebears, made his vigorous youth outstanding. Several times he had won the crown for being the first in assaulting the walls of enemy towns and acquiring many spoils. He had won equal civil honors. He so distinguished himself that he was made consul three times and was accompanied by the regal *fasces*. And in addition another special glory was added to the luster of these achievements: to him alone was awarded the sublime cognomen of Capitolinus. However, as he accumulated many honors, he gave little heed to an unfortunate ambition.

After Clusium was lost and the Roman strength had been broken at the Allia, the Gauls came to Rome, seized the city and massacred the senators. Only the Citadel of the Capitoline Hill was held by the Romans, and it was besieged. The Gauls discovered that they could enter the fortress by way of the Tarpeian Rock, for on that side, as if it were protected by nature, it was carelessly guarded. During a stormy night the Gauls attempted the ascent silently though with difficulty. By their quiet the climbers deceived the guards and the dogs alike, but they could not deceive the geese that were in the Citadel as a sacrifice to Juno, saved because they were scarce. Manlius was awakened by their clamor. He grabbed his weapons and after arousing the others attacked those who were climbing up. With a blow from the boss of his shield he pushed over a Gaul who was standing on top of the rock. The Gaul fell headlong on top of the others, and many of them came to an end with him in the river below. Then the Romans repelled many others hanging on the rocks, who toppled and fell into the river. And thus Manlius' skill and strength frustrated the hopes of the Gauls and the Citadel was defended. For this reason he received the highest praise from the military tribune and from everyone gifts according to the greatness of the time and occasion. It was here that the name Capitolinus was awarded him, as an eternal declaration from the Capitoline Hill that he had saved the Roman Republic's freedom.

In Italy Manlius' deed was regarded as outstanding and unique. Without doubt if he had not been corrupted by envy of the brilliance of another—and because of that he could not raise himself to a position higher than was befitting a citizen—it is easy enough to believe that one who began so vigorously, in the process of time would have earned the honor of dictatorships and the fame of triumphs. However, it was difficult for him to endure the glory that fell to Marcus Furius Camillus, and he in comparison belittled what he himself had received. By various means he captured the support of the Plebeians, so that he could seize the state which a little before he had defended lest it be seized by the Gauls. His mind was excited by anger and worse, envy.

Then many and divergent turmoils broke out. To allay the strife, Cornelius Cossus, a dictator, was recalled to the country from the land of the Volces. Cossus, after certain public disagreements with Manlius, sent out a lictor and ordered Manlius be put in prison, though the Plebeians complained about it. But what would seem to put his light under a shade, rather led to its increased brilliance. The Plebeians suffered his imprisonment very angrily, and after they had fiercely rebuked the Senators, many of them dressed themselves in mourning and appeared in public with unshaven beards and untrimmed hair; they kept vigil at the entrance of the jail. Thus they demonstrated their great faith in Manlius and brought light to him in the midst of his darkness. They would have done much more if he had repressed his inborn imprudence with as much strength as he had expressed his self-confidence and rash suspicions.

At last Fortune spurred her destructive force against him. The dictator Cossus had triumphed against the Volces and had been relieved of his office, and because of this the Plebeians were left with more freedom to move about. They went to the prison, and with great clamor threatened that, unless Manlius were freed, they would free him themselves. To quiet them, the Senate gave them what they sought: they ordered Manlius freed from his chains. But he was driven by the kind of pride that swells up the soul, and strove with all his might to do those things quickly which would be of use to his taking power. Both the Senators and the Tribunes of the people observed this, but they did not endure it with much equanimity. With universal consent, the Tribunes indicted Manlius for his deeds. Manlius, meanly clad, was accompanied by neither a Senator nor either of his brothers, Aulus or Titus, but was surrounded only by a crowd of the Plebeians. And when it seemed that he would be convicted easily of excessive desire for office (a crime), he first spoke at length, baring his chest marked with scars. He pointed out the Citadel of the Capitoline Hill that he had defended; he implored the help of the gods and the support of the Plebeians. He would not be condemned by the vote of the Plebeians, but was led outside the Flumentane Gate from where the Capitoline Hill could not be seen. There in the name of the Plebeians he was condemned as evil and ambitious, and was sentenced to be thrown from the Tarpeian Rock into the Tiber, even as he had done to the Gauls.

After he had vainly called on the help of the gods and the favor of the people, he suffered without delay the punishment he had meted out to the enemy, and was ignominiously driven over the precipice.

AGAINST THE FAITHLESSNESS
OF THE COMMON PEOPLE

The changeable nature of the crowd is even more dangerous to a ruler than envy.

I pray that those who have so much confidence in their own fortunes and superciliously raise their eyebrows at all other people come out of their ignorant darkness and think about Manlius, who knocked down the Gauls with his shield. He was praised to the sky by his soldiers, robed like a king, crowned in laurel, and borne in triumph to the Capitol by those he had defended. But in an instant everything was turned upside down. These people should see him then, dressed in rags, on his knees and weighed down by chains, condemned, waiting on the edge of the Tarpeian Rock for a blow from a lictor.

This event, so unpleasant in itself, would move them. Even if they believe in a sneering Fortune, the greatness of their name, their important family connections—but above all in the ingratitude of the common people— they would more wisely put aside any pride in their hearts.

To be sure it is doubtful which is more foolish, to be tormented by the envy of someone else's fortune, or to have faith in the applause of the multitude. Envy tortures, but the multitude deceives. The first drives a man to destroy others; the second destroys him by his own conceit. The one inflames the mind; the other mocks hope. But we have been considering the effect rather than the cause. Of course, envy should be restrained in the same way that an enemy of society should be put in chains. Nevertheless, no one should ever put his faith in the praises of the common people. It is in the nature of the multitude to be ever changeable and perverse, preferring always conjecture to truth, crying always for activity, then deserting in times of danger. The crowd follows where Fortune goes, serves her humbly, but rules severely. And after bestowing its gifts, it kills those unfortunates who had trusted it.

Although we have mentioned no other examples, it is enough to have seen Marcus Manlius, the protector of the people and their famous leader, who had in turn fixed all his hopes on them. They had honored him almost as a god, and while he was in prison, they took care of him. And by misfortune his horrible affliction began. He offered prayers to the gods and threatened the fathers of the city, but they finally took him away and while he was imploring their favor, they condemned him.

ABOUT ALEXANDER THE GREAT AND CALLISTHENES THE PHILOSOPHER

Alexander is very cruel to his teacher who tries to remind him of the truths of philosophy.

I had put down my pen when I saw Arisba, once King of Epirus, weeping and complaining, accusing Philip of Macedonia of great treachery. Driven by his desire for glory Philip seized the kingdom, and when Arisba was an old man, drove him into exile. In his place Philip put Alexander, the brother of his wife, Olympias. I would not have refused this king, the squalor of whose old age and the helplessness of whose misery easily persuaded me to include his complaint, if an even greater pity had not turned me from him. Not very far away Callisthenes followed silently, so disfigured and so filthy with gore that you would have thought him rather a mutilated body covered with blood and dirt and moving under its own power than a man who walked. By chance I heard his name and remembered suddenly that it was once a celebrated one among the schools of sacred philosophy. I was unable to hold back my tears, and promised him my pen against those who were cruel to him. Who is so callous that if he saw an honorable man, steeped in holy learning, strong of character, distinguished for a venerable name that Philosophy had bestowed on him, his appearance now deformed and maimed, his body covered with blood and filth, not because of his own deficiencies but because of the perversity of others—who, I say, could pass this man by and restrain his tears?

Ordinarily fame is accorded those favored by a distinguished ancestry, by royal forebears who performed admirable deeds; but in philosophy these things are of no importance. To a philosopher what do great renown or sceptered ancestors bring? Or the portraits of forefathers, or kings conquered or all the earth subdued? Not only does Philosophy disdain worldly honors; she traverses heaven itself, adorning it with a certain incomprehensible light. So to make Callisthenes greater we do not search out his ancestral line. His youth was spent in veneration at the altar of learning. Perhaps he listened to Socrates and Plato, who among mortals were actually divine treasure houses of heavenly wisdom. Without doubt he developed as a student endowed with great genius under Aristotle, the most famous of all philosophers. His reputation was already such that he had pupils to whom Aristotle, the master of natural science, revealed his secrets.

When Alexander of Macedonia organized his great expedition, he asked Aristotle, his teacher (doubtless engaged in more important tasks), to send one of his followers who could help him retain what he knew of his former learning and who could teach him the proofs of things he did not know. In addition, if perchance Alexander performed some deed worthy of being remembered, this teacher could record it. Wishing to please Alexander, the famous master, from among all the rest who were worthy both in talent and character of so great a ruler, chose as a friend and teacher for the campaign Callisthenes, outstanding for his honor and eloquence.

Certainly if philosophy is to be honored with its own eminence, it must be granted a great and illustrious purpose. Philosophy by its teaching should control the habits of those who command great armies and by its words should guide those who influence the great rulers. Fortune (always envious of anything outstanding) cannot wound Philosophy with her spears. But to impress those who care only for the outward appearance of the world, she directs her javelin against the great achievements of the philosopher. It happened that Alexander was prospering, and had already taken over many kingdoms. After he had conquered Darius and the Persian army, he acquired such great booty that he forgot he was a mortal being. He had the presumption to wish to be worshipped as a god by his followers according to the custom of the Persians. The well-informed Macedonians were unsympathetic to this, but of them all Callisthenes was the most antagonistic. Not only by his attitude but also with sharp reproofs he condemned the madness of the king as being both foolish and detestable. Indeed, this most honorable man remembered that recently Alexander had fallen into the frigid Cydnos River. When he contracted a near-mortal illness, he was cured not by his own divinity but by the grace of God and the efforts of physicians. Callisthenes knew that Alexander was again and again overcome by wine and anger, and he knew also that, like ordinary men, Alexander was burdened down with unhappiness and disturbed by very serious cares. These were circumstances quite foreign to any idea of divinity. Callisthenes knew that Alexander had been nourished on the sweet milk of Philosophy, reared in her holy lap and raised in her virtuous house. It was most unfitting that he—not a simple hireling, but one steeped in divine knowledge—should allow himself to be taken in by foolish untruths, should believe shallow fictions, or should worship any man, any creature, with the reverence due to God. It was even more blameworthy in Alexander, whose very life should serve as an example to those who observed him.

The steadfast philosopher could not be deterred from reminding Alexander of these facts. At last Alexander succumbed to the anger that was habitual with him, and resolved to punish the innocent man severely. He charged this man—who had occupied himself only in the contemplation of holiness—of conspiring against him with many others. By Alexander's order his eyes were dug out, his ears, nose, lips, hands, and feet cut off. Then this teacher of the king, robed according to his office, was led as an object of ridicule into the presence of the army which was aroused in anger against him. But these horrors did not yet satisfy the madness of the emperor. Callisthenes was enclosed in a cave, alone with a wild dog whose constant attacks allowed him no rest. Lysimachus, a young nobleman of Macedonia, took pity on him after these continual torments. He had frequently heard the principles of virtue and natural causation expounded by Callisthenes. To put an end to his torments in death, Lysimachus pretended to bring Callisthenes some food, but instead brought poison. And thus, after suffering these many outrages, endured because of the insanity of a single, wrathful youth, this foster child of Philosophy passed away.

You slothful in mind, tell me, I pray you, what are you doing to defend your own silly ideas? For was Fortune able to seize the castle of Philosophy? But what of your lengthy reposes, sumptuous feasts, golden robes, obscene lusts, habitual vices? These are your frivolous defenses against Fortune. What then can be said? Be stubborn no longer. Open the eyes of your intellect and see that only humility, the greatest of God's virtues, can weaken this monster. And put your confidence in Him who alone can unseat the powerful, and, whenever He wishes, can lift the poor from their depth.

ABOUT MARCUS ATILIUS REGULUS

*Regulus not only argued successfully against his
own life for the sake of his country, but
also kept his word to his enemies.*

Marcus Atilius Regulus, who must always be venerated
in the memory of mankind, was a Plebeian by origin,
from a family remarkable for its cheerful poverty yet
still honorable. The family possessed not quite four and
a half acres in the Popine region of the land, from which
by never-ending toil Atilius provided what meager
livelihood he could for himself and his children; but
he was by far more careful to cultivate faithfulness and
the other virtues than he was to cultivate his fields.

Because of his outstanding constancy he was named
consul of the Romans, who were pursuing a very severe
war against the Carthaginians, a nation superior to all
others at that time. With his associate, Manilius, he
embarked in a fleet that had been prepared. Although
from a farmer he was made an admiral and commander-
in-chief, he was not ignorant of military affairs, for with
great force Manilius and he attacked the Sicilians on
the well-known islands of Lipara and Malta. Then in
the vicinity of Sicily they put to flight Hamilcar, the
commander-in-chief of the Punic army, and Hannibal,
the admiral of the Punic fleet, after a naval battle in
which they captured almost all of the enemy ships.
Then invading Africa, they captured the city of Clipea
by force of arms, received the surrender of some of the
other cities, and destroyed still others. Finally, by a
decree of the Senate, Atilius was made sole commander-

in-chief. He ordered Manilius to return to Rome with the fleet filled with booty taken from the Carthaginians, and Atilius remained alone in Africa. Eager to bring the war to a close he attacked the enemy with his victorious army and penetrated into Africa. Then he learned of the death of the steward to whom he had entrusted the care of his little farm so that his wife and children might be sustained. Another farmer who could substitute for the steward was absent. In no way haughty because of the splendor either of his position or of his victories, he sought a successor so that from private labor rather than from public acclaim he could support his family.

Oh, the illustrious sign of the conscientious spirit! He rejected the highest power so that he would not be forced to provide for his children dishonorably. The Senate took care of his domestic affairs, however, and ordered him to continue what he had begun. He accomplished his mission, and established a camp not far from the Bragada River. Here he killed a snake of astounding size, and, as proof of the wonder, sent the skin to Rome. Later he met an army, led by the two Hasdrubals, which consisted of a great number of well-armed Numidians. After a sharp fight, Atilius put them to flight. Finally Hamilcar, more formidable than the other two, was recalled from Sicily, and Atilius had an encounter with him. Fortune cast Hamilcar down like the others, and this defeat so weakened the forces of the Carthaginians that Atilius, in order to make peace, imposed the conditions of surrender on them.

This man, who previously had been only a farmer, was now carried to the highest pinnacle. Not long before he had carried a hoe and a rake; now he carried Scipio's ivory baton. The man who had led sheep now led an army. He subdued cities, fleets, and important captains;

he ordered out lictors equipped with axes and rods, he who was more used to turning over the soil. What more can be said? A great triumph was prepared for Atilius, now adorned with the laurel crown of Phoebus and the golden robes of Jupiter, and he was given a golden chariot with white horses. The great doors of the Capitol were opened to him, and prayers and supplications were addressed to him almost as if he were one of the gods.

But now Fortune, as if she regretted his past glories, not only stole back everything, but also converted what had been good to evil. For when the Carthaginians saw that the conditions of peace which Atilius had imposed could not be tolerated, they turned to help outside their country, among whom were the Spartans under Xanthippus. Immediately he was made the leader of the war. Xanthippus took the initiative against Atilius, for Fortune had changed with the Roman commander. Not only did Xanthippus defeat the Romans in a very great slaughter, but also he captured Atilius himself. Burdened down with chains Atilius was made a comic spectacle for the Carthaginians, and then thrown into a darkened prison where he languished in filth and squalor.

How the end mocked the beginning! In the robes of a general he left the city of Rome, but conquered, he was locked in a Carthaginian prison. While he was a conqueror, he ruled leaders; conquered, he was led by slaves. In triumph he seemed to hold all the honors of the Capitol in his hand as a reward for what he had accomplished. What followed then was the darkness of a prison and the melancholy of servitude. It seemed as if his name, once celebrated, became cursed. But that is the way it is: Fortune changes a person's lot, and uses his possessions according to her law.

Yet though she tried with all her strength, much that

belonged to Atilius she was unable to take away. In chains a greater renown came to him than to a king on his throne, for while Atilius was conquered and spending his life in darkness, the power of the Carthaginians was challenged and broken by the Romans, now in Africa, now in Sicily. Finally it diminished enough so that the Romans could seek peace. The Carthaginians had a great desire to take back their young men held captive by the Romans. Atilius had been in prison for five years, and the Carthaginians suggested that he go to Rome with their delegates. By returning him they thought they could get their own youths in exchange, and after they took a promise from him that if the plan was not successful he would return to prison, they released him.

Atilius went to Rome, and with the consent of the Senate explained the purpose of the mission. Then he asked that he be allowed to speak not about his own affairs but those of the nation. He said that it would accomplish very little for the republic to give back healthy young men in exchange for an old man, his usefulness over, in order to obtain a peace with the army of a city weary and exhausted.

This was a noble action on the part of Atilius which demonstrated his integrity; but even a greater one was to follow. After he had given his counsel, which was the best advice for the republic, his friends and relations intreated him to deceive an enemy that was faithless and impious. He could be free to enjoy the company of his own people in joyous liberty. But he, in his constancy, spurned this suggestion. He would rather return to the enemy, who now was infuriated by his action, than break faith in anything or violate a sacred oath in any way. And so, returning to Carthage from Rome, he went back to prison.

What can we think of so perfect a fidelity except that the everlasting honor of eternal fame is reserved among the gods for this extraordinary man, in compensation for the felicity lost by the guilt of Fortune. His reputation is the brighter as he was stronger in his virtue. The Carthaginians on the other hand had learned what advice he had given the Senate, and were so madly inflamed that they contrived the most savage kinds of torture and death for him. They deprived him of sleep, cut the lids from his eyes, then placed him on a plank from the surface of which, I believe, many sharp points pressed into the defenseless old man. The continuous agony and never-ending loss of blood combined with his inability to fall into a natural sleep brought about his death among these many sharp barbs. Oh death, by far more illustrious than the life of many men, with the greatest praise you have borne the spirit of this vital person to the other world.

AGAINST THOSE WHO DO NOT LOVE THEIR COUNTRY ENOUGH

This kind of man prefers wealth and is never true to his word, or even to a sworn oath.

Why do I wonder that the Roman Empire was only bounded by the sea when I contemplate such citizens as this? The power of Fortune was nothing against them, and for those who wish to see it, this is the proof that where virtue is, Fortune has no power. If the virtuous person for a time is given to license, then immediately his excess is held in check by strength of another kind; and what evil occurred because of his negligence is

redressed because of his diligence. To illustrate what
I wish to say, the Camilli, the Papirii, the Scipiones,[1]
and many others have been able to perform very
memorable deeds which seem to overshadow those of
the unfortunate Atilius. In virtue and in loyalty, however, Cato himself is not more distinguished.

What other citizen anywhere, finding himself surrounded by the riches of Sicily and Africa, surrounded
by the enormous booty gathered daily by his soldiers,
would still keep his hand from what belonged to the
nation and not put aside some little thing for his indi-
gent household? I submit neither Curius nor Fabricius,
not Lucius Bestia nor Aemilius Scaurus,[2] nor above all
Crassus, that very great swallower of gold. And to these,
if honor did not forbid me, I would like to add some
of my own countrymen who think it is virtuous to go
out on some military expeditions only for the profit
they will get from pillaging, from sacking both holy
places and unhallowed ones, from plundering anything
that has been destroyed, and all the while thinking they
are above punishment.

For those who understand the allure of avarice enough
has been said. Above all, I wish that those who want
to be first in acclaim but last in effort had heard Atilius
addressing the Senate, pressing the good of the state
against his own liberty. Then, if their avarice would
let them, they might be conscious of their citizenship,
as Atilius was, that most constant of men, who, though
he had experienced the ferocity of torture and prison,

---

[1] The Camilli were best known for Furius Camillus, who,
in 396 B.C., helped unify Italy by conquering a northern tribe,
the Veians. The Papirii boasted of Papirius Cursor who gave
all his spoils to the treasury; the Scipiones are, of course, the
great family eventually awarded the surname of Africanus.
[2] The first two were noted for their frugality, the latter for
their luxury.

without a second thought offered himself to death for the salvation of his country. Those people are detestable who, in their enormous ambition, gather all riches and honors but shirk any public responsibility. They burden themselves for private ends. They are not afraid to lie about being poor. Everybody knows that they never risk their blood or tax their minds for the good of their country, and without any embarrassment they refuse their country even a small part of their wealth. They have enough so their daughters offer the biggest dowries to their suitors; enough so they celebrate marriage festivities and revelries with great splendor; enough so they decorate their houses not, let me say, like ordinary persons, but like kings; enough so they deck their wives in expensive dresses, regal crowns, and bracelets of gold and jewels; enough so they feed blooded horses, falcons, and dogs; but they do not have enough to help the needs of the country.

Oh, you fools, what will become of you? What good will your own riches be, your marriage unions and your power if your country is in danger? Who will curb the violence of the criminal, who will prevent crimes, who will make the laws if subsidy for the state comes to an end? This is the kind of citizen who does not consider, or rather does not wish to consider, that we are born first for our country and after that for ourselves.

So that I do not speak only of those who deserve reproach, let us consider the faithfulness of this outstanding man, whose integrity was so great that not by the tears of his children, not by the prayers of his friends, not by the charms of his home-land, not by his love of life, nor by the terror of immediate punishment was he to be shaken from the oath that he had made. Alas, there is hardly anything men care less about today. A thousand promises are made which are disavowed for the least excuse, for lies, for general convenience, not only by tricks of interpretation but also by facetious cavilling.

But whoever you are, by what idea, by what foolish audacity will you pray God that He grant you goodness, He who is the highest and whole truth, when you have given false witness and fake bond? You have denied His name in levity and laughter, and you love only little things. Do you think that if you have tried to deceive God, who sees all things, men will prove faithful to you? Do you think that I exaggerate your example? You who take the name of God in vain, will I believe your word? You who did so much that in you God was a liar? You are wrong. It was not enough for you to observe that great nobleman, Atilius, who preferred to give himself up to die rather than deceive his gods, who he affirmed were trifling.

But so we do not parade each of the outstanding virtues of this poor and equally distinguished man, Marcus Atilius, let me say that these nobles surrounded by luxuries should be ashamed, they should be ashamed who have places of trust in the cities, when they see a spirit so pre-eminent in virtue hidden under a skin hardened by dust and tanned by the heat of the sun, a virtue under the hand calloused by the hoe and plow, under clothes made only from the hides of farm animals. His true light obscures their false glitter. Let them not belittle him or condemn him with mockery and scoffing, as if by so doing they could overcome his tremendous virtue. Those who think they can disparage him are wrong. While they condemn him they actually praise him. I do not think that any greater misfortune can fall on a man renowned for his virtue than to be praised by the idle.

ABOUT HANNIBAL,
KING OF CARTHAGE

Hannibal conquered Spain and Italy, but died in
a strange land, betrayed by a friend.

As soon as I had finished the unfortunate history of
Atilius, Hannibal, the powerful Phoenician, the great
scourge of our country, Italy, brought himself to our
attention, condemning the snares of Fortune with a sad
and pensive voice. Because his accomplishments were
tremendous, I had to address myself to writing about
him concisely, as I had written about the others.

Hannibal was descended from many generations of
the most noble Carthaginian leaders and was the son
of the renowned ruler, Hamilcar. Thus he was born
into the world as the permanent enemy of the Romans.
Still only nine years old, while his father made a sacrifice, he swore that as soon as his age would permit
him, he would be a foe to the name of Rome. Nor did
this pledge lack effect; for within three years his father
had died, and with the greatest promise for the future,
he took up arms under Hasdrubal. When Hasdrubal was
killed by a barbarian, Hannibal took his place on the
spot. Fighting hard he brought some of the Spanish
people under his power, and after their long siege
against law and order, he massacred the Saguntines.

He was encouraged by a vision he had during his
sleep that he would achieve a victory in Italy. He
crossed the Iberus River, and with the permission of
the Gauls crossed the Pyrenees and arrived at the Alps.
Almost impassable, they were rough and very difficult

because of the harassment and robbery of the inhabitants often occupying the passes, as well as the falling snow and the ice that made the route slippery and hard. They drove off the inhabitants; they pressed down the snow, and with vinegar and fire, they broke the hard rocks. He had lost almost half of his troops by cold and starvation. Over the cliffs he lost almost all his elephants, a great many of his supply animals, and most of his military equipment. Still he overcame his difficulties with what was left. As some authorities believe, he came down into Italy in the vicinity of the Taurines,[3] which is watered by the Po River. Here he refreshed his troops in the quiet of the place and on its abundant food.

Hannibal descended to Ticinum and defeated an army under Gnaeus Scipio, the consul, who fled wounded. With the same good fortune he proceeded to the River Trebbia where he defeated Sempronius, the other consul. With great effort he crossed the Apennines and continued down to Tuscany. Not far from Faesulae, with his army, he crossed a river swollen with the rains of the previous day. He occupied the whole plain, but the army was led into a place that was wet and marshy. Throughout the many days, most of the men became infected with the cold, and when the supply animals died, it caused a great disruption. A leader, who in the midst of the dampness presided over the only elephant that survived, lost one eye because of the cold and the marshy air. But the army overcame these difficulties with their strong morale. They left this uncomfortable and damp location, and regained their normal strength as soon as they came to Lake Trasumenus, where they inflicted a severe defeat on Flaminius, the consul, and slaughtered him.

[3] The area of modern Turin.

After this occurred, the cities and allies of the Romans went to Hannibal and offered him aid, brought provisions, a sufficiency of everything. Then far and wide, as almost no one opposed them, the victorious army plundered throughout Italy, but they were fooled for a year by the delays of Quintus Fabius Maximus. The Romans thought this was a technique for easing the war but not for winning it, and on the insistence of Terentius Varro, the consul, they struck at Cannae, where more by his dexterity than by force of arms, Hannibal achieved victory. The slaughter crushed the strength of the Romans. Aemilius, the consul, was killed, Varro fled to Venusia, the army was slaughtered in the debacle, and many Senators, consuls, and praetors were killed. To the vanquished there remained scarcely any hope of deliverance or of saving their freedom. If Hannibal had then followed the counsel of Maharbal, he would have conquered the republic of Rome, but the victor himself was presumptuous and thought he was safe in taking the city. He would first show the Carthaginians how things were, and as evidence of the victory he collected the rings from the hands of the dead Romans and sent three bushels of them to Carthage.

This was the pinnacle of his joy. Fortune raised him up to this point. Whatever he would do in the future influenced either the sudden change of his prosperity or contributed to its decline. After he had captured Capua (at that time a powerful city) because of the surrender of its citizens, he led the army into it to spend the winter there. He thought that by doing this he would make the conquered Campanians fearful, but, on the contrary, he only lessened by a great deal the strength of his army. They became weakened by the abundance of goods and the freedom of the Campanian women with the Africans and Spaniards who had shat-

tered the Roman army. Those whom he led in at the
beginning of winter did not seem to be those whom he
led out. When they left Capua, suddenly they were
closely surrounded by the Romans and moved around
with varying consequences trying to free themselves.
Hannibal moved the army up to the third milestone
from the city that had now recovered its breath. It
seemed to the ancients that at this juncture the gods
fought for the city, for there was such a downpour
that twice the Carthaginians had to give up their
attack. Disappointed in their effort, they moved about
in the Italian provinces. Despairing of doing this alone,
Hannibal recalled his brother Hasdrubal, a very famous
commander, from Spain. He would confer with Hasdrubal about the victory that had such a good start,
but before Hannibal saw him, he learned that while
Hasdrubal was coming, he was conquered in an unfortunate battle with Livius Salinator at the Metaurus
River, and was killed. In this blow Hannibal recognized
that he and his soldiers were exhausted and beaten as
far as the opportunities of fighting were concerned. Then
he learned that the war which he brought into Italy,
Scipio had transferred to Africa.

When Scipio arrived there, he captured Syphax and
in many defeats smashed the Carthaginians who were
almost sealed within their own walls. Hannibal was
recalled to defend his country. He knew that he would
return to Africa with much greater shame than the
honor he had when he conquered Italy. He came back
almost an old man, though he had left a youth. He
abandoned Italy, which he thought he had obtained
by his occupation of sixteen years.

He battled with Scipio and was conquered with the
greatest loss of citizens. Constrained by necessity, the
Carthaginians then came under Roman rule, and Han-

nibal saw that he came to Carthage when a little before
he had hoped that he would come to Rome. But when
he discovered that Gnaeus Servilius, who had been
sent by the Romans to Carthage, had been killed, Hannibal secretly loaded his goods into a ship and went
into exile. And with a few followers he who a little
before had been a leader of armies, fled to Antioch, now
preparing for war against the Romans. At first he was
received graciously but then held in suspicion, for he
began to arouse the envy of the leaders.

Afterward Antioch was defeated by Rome, and Scipio
laid down the conditions of peace. Warned ahead of
time about this, Hannibal went to Crete with all his
belongings. Here, in order to take away any worries that
the inhabitants might have about him, and also to
protect his life, he secretly filled some jugs with lead
then deposited them in the Temple of Diana, as if he
were giving all his treasure to be preserved by the
public. But all his gold he liquefied and poured into
empty statues which, like household gods, he carried
with him. In this way the citizens had no suspicions
of him, and for a very short space of time he lived
quietly in private.

Then he learned that Prusias, King of Bithynia [4] and
an enemy of the Romans, would make war against
Eumenes, King of Pergamum, an ally of Rome, and
Hannibal went to Bithynia. Guided by his advice, Prusias
won some battles, but the war was settled by Roman
envoys sent to Eumenes and Prusias, and Titus Quintius
Flaminius demanded Hannibal. Because of this demand,
immediately Prusias sent his soldiers, who completely
surrounded Hannibal's dwelling place and took care

[4] Bithnyia was on the southern shore of the Black Sea, along
the Bosphorus in present-day Turkey. Pergamum is modern
Bergamo, Lombardy.

that no one was able to escape. But Hannibal felt that Flaminius' arrival meant death to him, and knew that only a few people had confidence in the king; so he fled to a very secret gate of his house. When he discovered that the gate was already held by the guards, he took poison that was always at hand to escape any desperate situation. Invoking the gods of hospitality on the head of the king and against the changed customs of the Romans, he drained the cup and died not long after. He was buried in Lybissa, a city of Bithynia.

The man who occupied Spain, who conquered the inaccessible Alps, who overcame the rigors of ice and snow and the storms of the Apennines, who endured the marshes, who often trampled the land of the Samnites, the Lucani, and the Bruttii,[5] who time and again had conquered praetors, consuls, and armies, who humbled the arms of Rome and—to the fright of Rome itself—for a long time occupied almost all of Italy, was now forced to give obedience to kings, a helpless old man, deprived of his ancestral gods and his titles, half-blind, an exile. And then, because of their deceit, his wearied spirit was driven out by poison. And as he came so disgracefully to his end, it demonstrates more clearly what is the strength of man, the mobility of Fortune, and the nature of perishable things.

[5] These were different tribes of Italy, where Hannibal fought his campaigns.

ABOUT PRUSIAS,
THE KING OF BITHYNIA

*A great king conspired against his own son and
lost everything in the attempt.*

God, avenger of sin, was with me as if He were my
counselor, and made me turn my attention toward
Prusias, advancing sad and plaintive, his eyes filled with
tears, though there were many sorrowing who were
milling around me on all sides. Perhaps, when I have
explained his griefs, I can prove that he suffered justly,
because he broke his promise to Hannibal. So therefore
I left the others and turned to his misfortunes.

If we have faith in the ancient writers, we must grant
that, without doubt, the kings of Bithynia were of an
exceptionally worthy line, among whom Prusias did
not have little excellence. After the wars between him
and Eumenes, King of Pergamum, were settled and
Hannibal had died because of his treachery, he took
a stepmother for his son Nicodemus and by her had
other sons. From these he wished to provide a succession
for the kingdom, and in his mind conceived the most
evil of plans that to his grandeur brought meanness, to
his splendor, tarnish. To his courtiers he revealed his
plan, which was to have his son Nicodemus killed while
he was away. Nicodemus heard of this through friends
and returned, incensed at his father's iniquity. Surrounded by a group of his trustworthy friends, he caught
his father unawares and easily drove him from the
kingdom.

Prusias had turned the good will of all the princes

against him, and in misery went into exile with only a few attendants, neither aided nor honored; then Fortune was harsh against him, for after a time even those attendants left him. And so, the lonely and destitute old man, his life insecure, was distressed by chagrin, both in the memory of his crime and the loss of his honor. For his own safety he moved only at night, and to avoid ignominy he took another name, begging his bread and seeking the wilds. During the day he withdrew into the darkness.

But who can easily escape the hands of kings? Prusias could certainly not hide nor evade the wrath of Nicodemus. After a long time he was discovered, and in his death he paid for the evil that he had conceived, and the memory of Hannibal was revenged. He was killed with no less cruelty than he had planned against Nicodemus. And so while he tried to conspire against his son, this unfaithful king lost the splendor of a famous kingdom, reward due to honor, and his own life.

A CONVERSATION BETWEEN
FORTUNE AND THE AUTHOR

*The author defends his style to Fortune, and she
aids him in choosing some worthy subjects.*

I was taking up my pen again after a very short rest
when suddenly there appeared that horrible monster,
administrator of all mortal affairs, Fortune. Oh God,
how tall she was, what an extraordinary appearance!
I did not say anything. I was afraid of her looks, for
her eyes were burning and menacing, her aspect over-
powering. Her twisted hair hung in front of her face,
and I think she had a hundred hands and arms, a dress
of many colors, a voice like rough iron. I could not see
how she moved her feet. Alarmed, I waited for what
she might want. She fixed her eyes on me and said:

"Madman, why do you waste yourself on such foolish
labor? You go running around with calamitous speed,
now from east to west following the sun, now from
the Arctic to the Antarctic. Those persons who were
raised up to the stars by my hands you pursue, sometimes one, sometimes another. Then you go into the
lower world and describe their fall with your pen as
if with just a few words you might reveal our very
weighty labors. You think that you will provoke the
mind of man to know itself. But you are wrong. For
who, except you, does not know that deeds are more
powerful than words? I leave many things destroyed,
and by these means pointing out the laws of our game,
I try in vain to educate man. I am always busy; I make

the highest into the lowest, and the lowest I raise to where he equals the highest. I go everywhere, sometimes threatening, sometimes pleading. Nor do I visit only regal houses or the sacrosanct palaces of emperors, which, for the most part, you are examining. But I also seek out the poor man's hovel, the shepherd's hut, and the fisherman's cabin. Then when everybody has his eyes on these, I find someone who is weighed down by his calamities to whom I again show my pleasure. I have always been received with great hope, and I laugh at it.

"But what do you think you are doing telling me about our efforts so briefly? Since the labors of others failed, why do you take on this solitary task?" Now that she was quiet, I began to get my courage back.

"I know there is nothing permanent under the sun, because your vacillation is indefatigable. I undertook this task, such as it is, of my own free will so that when I pass away, my name will not be closed up in my tomb with my body, and it would seem that I only lived for my stomach like a wild animal. I am not so slow-witted that I do not know there are many things that furnish an abundance of material for writing. For example: to reveal the glory and the miraculous greatness of the Omnipotent Father of all things, through Whom all creation was made and Who is one deity in three persons; or to disclose the secrets of all-powerful nature discovered by skillful investigation; or to discover the infinite splendors of law.

"But the man is judged prudent who places on his shoulders only what he can bear. I know that I do not have the feathers of a bird by the aid of which I could penetrate the Heavens to view the secrets of God. Then I could reveal these sights to mortal man. By the grace of God it was not granted to me that I see these things,

nor was the grandeur of words, the depth of understanding given to me that, though flying through the
skies, I would still be able to disclose the truth to
posterity. I plainly confess, also, that I do not have
the clear insight by which I could reach the cause of
creation.

"What is left for my purpose is that I come back to
you, the source of much of human affairs. Here great
poets and famous historians drew unfailing material
for their singing and writing. And while I stood in their
presence and, full of wonder, observed their many and
varied works, I was driven to a higher purpose. Knowing
my powers, however (and since no one had an objec-
tion), I took a small part of their works which seemed,
according to my understanding, suitable to my labors,
and placed these small parts under the hammer of my
talent. This is the method I have employed until now.

"But now you criticize the awkwardness of my style
too much, as if, because of it, I could not move the
hearts of my readers. It is the height of stupidity to
deny that a style based on Cicero's careful eloquence
is much more polished than crude. But sometimes his
eloquence did not lack the effect of being crude, because
it was the means by which the common people of
Rome were led from the sacred mount back to the city
and into the favor of the Senators. But the people better
understood Cicero's faith than his eloquence. As for me,
for those who recognize good style, I have not put
much labor into this work. But for anyone else, it is
enough if they understand that other powerful rulers
have fallen from on high, and that they, too, can fall
in the same way at some time. Therefore, with my
feeble style, I think I accomplished much with these
rulers. You, by the thunder of your destruction, do not
warn them but strike them senseless. To be sure, we are

taught by experience; but if we spur a horse too much, we do not speed it on its way but very often make it go back. If we strike it with a supple stick, however, the horse obeys us. Persons who cannot be changed are not moved by torture; but for the docile, soft words are no less useful than blows. The soft sound of words very often assuages the ferocious animosity of an Achilles, when neither the crash of armor, the Trojan strength of arms, nor the wrath of Agamemnon could ever move him. But I know that when you make a turn of your wheel, you can take anything from the earth. I pray you that by your grace you will favor this work which I have begun, so that my name, which is unknown today, by your brilliance will become illustrious to posterity."

Now her expression was softer, and smiling, she said: "Because the understanding of man is not able to penetrate into our designs, you think Fortune is inexorable, indiscreet, and blind. This is the way you paint me on the walls of your buildings. You are blinded by your own insatiable desire, and think that I do not know how much you have written that is opposed to what I am. Recall, if you can, what slanders, what blasphemies, what insults you once wounded me with! Sometimes you call me stupid, then barren, now envious, murderous, hostile, and a cruel stepmother because I have not immediately satisfied your silly desires. What is even more painful to me, you have gotten a good laugh hearing that I was conquered by Poverty. Now, as if I could be fooled like a simple country girl with lies and flattery, you bend your knee and implore my help. I know and know well what you are thinking. You have faith in my powers; whatever my mind may be, you have changed it and changed my plan. Now I praise your task and I praise your ability, and as long as you pursue your idea which you have begun so skillfully, my favor will not fail you, and your name and that of Certaldo will be numbered among the famous names of antiquity.

"So you may believe this, I will give you a start before I leave. I know that you are uncertain, worried as to whom you should select of the many persons in misery who are presenting themselves to you. Perhaps Lucius Apuleius Saturninus, of whose insolence and audacity at the time of the Roman assembly there is evidence. Very often he alone made the fields of Mars flow with Roman blood, and the speech he made to the leaders assembled in the Senate, who were murmuring against him, will be praised unless you are silent about it. Or there is Glaucus, one of the guards who was made a consul. After achieving great honor he was besieged in the Capitol, and by an insurrection was driven to surrender to the Plebeians, whom he had often led as tribune. They killed him with cudgels and stones, and his head, cut off from his body in disgrace, was carried through the mob.

"Or perhaps Marcus Livius Drusus; though he was of an especially noble family, his pride, ambition, and perfidy must be detested. When you consider his deeds, you will be astonished to see that as a Quaestor in Asia he refused the insignia of office and said that he, himself, was more eminent than the insignia and that there was nothing that seemed better than himself. You would be amazed also that he said he put aside everything he shared with ordinary men except the sky and the earth. Finally, with his face lowered, he complained how his evil was discovered and that Nabdasam, Prince of Mauritania (who had taken money from Boccus, King of the Moors), had him thrown in the path of an elephant. You will discover that he found a shameful death in the midst of the people.

"Then you may see the raving Syrus, the shepherd

Antonius, and above all the gladiator Spartacus who because of my favor escaped from the compound for slaves and drove bands of them to victory over their Roman leaders. Some of them were not afraid to put on the robes of kings and others to employ the signs of the emperor. Nevertheless, the gladiator was finally killed, and the others received their punishment on the cross.

"These persons are proof of the strength of our power, yet I want you to include in your work one after the other those whom I shall call to your attention."

Without a minute's hesitation this regal woman made Marius of Arpinum appear in front of my eyes. He was completely distressed, still spattered with the blood of Roman citizens, very somberly dressed, his hair snarled, his beard filthy, and his face covered with mournful tears. Fortune spoke:

"The man you see before you I raised almost from the lowest dregs of camp followers all the way to become consul seven times. I rewarded him with every distinction, and to no man who was given triumphs in his time were they more welcome. And because he received rewards worthy of his excessive ambition, you will be able to use him as the best example of the world's instability."

The second one followed next. The instant I saw him, I knew him to be Pompey the Great, though he did not say anything. Oh, what a piteous and tender sight! He was still wet with the sea at Egypt and sooty with the ashes of the smoldering fragments of ships. He seemed scarcely able to hold up his head. Fortune led in the third with his venerable face and said:

"The man you see is that very extraordinary person, Marcus Tullius Cicero, the Prince of Roman eloquence, one of the guardians of philosophy, a celebrated man with whose destiny you are familiar. Content merely

to place him before your eyes, I will be silent about
both his successes and his calamities. You may write
as seems best to you about this man and the others."

Having said what she wished, she vanished into thin
air. I thought over what I had seen and heard, and felt
that I had to yield to her commands; and so, to keep
the order of the stories which Fortune had selected, I
begin with Marius.

ABOUT GAIUS MARIUS
FROM ARPINUM

*A great general was driven by envy of his rival
to the slaughter of his own people.*

According to the writings of the ancients, Arpinum was
a city of the Volces that was by no means unimportant,
and here Gaius Marius, his father a carpenter, had his
origin. As some writers believe, while a youth of some
years, he followed his father to the military camps. When
it seemed that he had experience according to his age,
and his body was strong enough for soldiery, he went
to Rome. His diligence, his skill at arms, and his worthi-
ness were easily recognized, and he attained the rank
of military tribune,[1] as well as other offices.

But he was implacable in mind when urged by a
driving eagerness. After he had been very successful
with affairs in Africa, the favorable portents of the
sacrifices of Haruspex [2] persuaded him to come to Rome

---

[1] There were six of these in a legion; they correspond roughly
to a regimental commander, except that the tribunes kept their
commmand only two months.

[2] A legendary soothsayer of the Etruscans, whose name came
to be used generically.

and seek the office of consul. Although he lacked the
social rank of his predecessors to obtain so great an
appointment, still hatred of the nobility was now so
severe among the Plebeians that not only did he obtain
the consulate as he wished, but also, by the consent of
all the Plebeians, was assigned the province of Numidia
that Metellus had governed for a long time. Within a
year he accomplished everything with skill and zeal that
for several years the nobles, corrupted by gold, had
not been able to do: he captured the king, Jugurtha.
This brilliant victory earned him so splendid a triumph
in the city that Metellus and the other nobles despised
him even more. But neither his character nor his fortune
held back his progress. Because of an action so celebrated and advantageous to the republic, the people
seemed to place all their hope in him.

The Cymbri, the Teutones, the Tigurini, and other
barbarian tribes were driven from their countries,[3] and
their armies were creating havoc, threatening the reputation of Rome with destruction. By this time they had
conquered three Roman leaders, put their armies to
flight, and seized their camps. In three columns they
crossed the Alps that protected Italy. Marius was sent
out against them, and Fortune favored him. At Aquae
Sextiae,[4] the scene of their first encounter, he defeated
them. The army of the Teutones came down in all their
great power, and Marius captured their fleeing king,
Teutoboc, a tall, very proud man, whom he kept in
chains for his triumph.

Then Marius turned his army against the Cymbri
who were in their camp at Caudium,[5] and with like
gratification defeated them in two battles. In the first

[3] What is now Southern France and Switzerland.
[4] Near Aix-en-Provence.
[5] A small town on the pass near Benevento.

he fought with great severity against the men, and there was a tremendous slaughter. Their king, Beleus, who had fought very courageously, fell among the soldiers. The second battle was fought against the women. When Marius had refused their request to become Vestal Virgins, they arranged their wagons into a barricade. Then, after they had suffocated their own infants, these fierce women, lugging their spears, arranged themselves in battle formation and held out for some time. When they saw that their efforts were vitiated by the troops of Marius, they found death by killing one another or by hanging, and to the victors they left only cadavers. Marius now had victories over two of the tribes and would have moved against the Tigurini, had he not heard through various sources that they were scattered and had fled through the passes of Noricum.[6] So he returned to Rome to the tumultuous enthusiasm of the Plebeians and entered the Capitol in a great triumph resulting from his victories; in testimony to the god, Liber (as was customary), he drank from a flask rather than a cup. Why should I enumerate this man's many accomplishments? By the gift of Fortune he was elevated to six consulates at this time, and being raised to continual eminence did not quench his thirst for glory but increased it.

It was perhaps thought, not without reason, that Fortune, who had thus far favored him, had changed her attitude to one of indignation. That year it was decreed for the consul, Lucius Sulla, to make war against Mithradates. Marius took this decree very painfully, not so much because the commission was given to Sulla, but more because it was not given to him. He began to oppose it by the help of the Sulpician law,

[6] Between Northern Italy and Bavaria.

which prohibited anyone absent being appointed to a province. Sulla was delayed with his army then, by chance, in Campania, opposing the rest of the allies in war. On hearing this he was aroused, and suddenly turned his army against Rome and the followers of Marius. He arrived there with the greatest speed, burning his way by fire. With a double column he entered the Equiline Gate and the Colline Region, and as victor occupied the Capitoline Citadel. Marius fled to the marshes at Minturnae [7] and hid there. But he was captured, all covered with mud, by those who followed him there, and given over to the inhabitants at Minturnae to be put in prison. On Sulla's order a certain Cymbrian, a very savage slave was sent to kill him. When Marius arose in his presence, albeit Marius was old and defenseless, by an authority coming, I believe, from his natural majesty, he actually overawed the Cymbrian so that the latter dared do nothing against him. It really happened, I think, that the one who overcame the King of the Cymbri was still not killed by a member of the same people. This slave stared at Marius transfixed, and Marius took advantage of the occasion to escape from his prison. For a short time he stayed at the home of Phania, a woman of Minturnae.

Guided by the prophetic signs he had seen on a mule, he set sail for Africa. Here his recent mishaps had not obscured his former reputation. He easily raised an army of various sorts of men, and, joining with Cornelius Cinna, he returned to Italy where he had been declared an enemy by the Senate. He divided his army into four columns, entered the city, and began an enormous slaughter of the Roman people. The head of the consul, Gnaeus Octavius, was cut off and put on the Rostra.

[7] An area between what is now Formia and Cassino.

Cornelius Merula, a priest of Jupiter, gave up his spirit in the Capitol before the Temple of Jupiter itself. Crassus and his son were slaughtered in his own house. Catulus suffocated in smoke and thus escaped the hands of his adversaries. Bebius, Numitorius, and many others were dragged by their executioners through the midst of the Forum.

Shall I list the names of all those who were slaughtered, those who fled, those who were exiled? Their blood and their wretchedness resulted in Marius' putting on the robe of the consulate for the seventh time. Fortune, however, would not allow him to see the end of his office, nor to exercise it in peace. The Senators who had fled the massacre pleaded with Sulla to return from the war against Mithradates to put an end to the madness of Marius. Although he had only weakened the strength of Mithradates, still he laid aside what he had begun and returned. What destruction, what deaths, what conflagrations his arrival brought on would be too lengthy to describe, though it is not outside our purpose. The followers of Marius were conquered in several encounters, and after many of his captains and soldiers had been killed, Sulla entered the city as the victor. His followers went everywhere about the city and killed whomever they wished. While I still will not mention any others, there was Marcus Marius, brother of Marius, the general, at the tomb of Catalus, or as others are wont to say, he was butchered outside the goat house belonging to the Lutatius family. His eyes were torn out, his hands cut off, his legs and other parts of his body were cut up, and his spirit left him only after the greatest suffering in mind and body. Afterward his head was cut off and sent to Praeneste [8] where Gaius Marius

[8] Modern Palestrina.

had fled. When he saw this, already broken by adversity, he was seized by complete desperation. And so that he would not fall alive into the hands of Lucretius who was besieging him, Marius agreed to a mutual death with Telesinus. Rushing violently at him, Marius killed Telesinus with his blow but was himself scarcely wounded. He offered his neck to a slave for a blow, and thus put an end to his achievement and to his sanguine old age. But still the power of Fortune's antagonism continued, and Sulla's ferocity was so great that he even ordered Marius' entombed body disinterred. He had what was left of the body taken from its coffin and thrown into the depths of the river.

A FEW WORDS ABOUT NOBILITY

True nobility is not inherited but comes from the practice of virtue.

Thus the life of Marius is a special example of the instability of Fortune, but I believe it is no less a proof of true nobility. Actually, I suggest that nobility is nothing more than a glorious splendor, shining in the eyes of those directly beholding it, because of an elegance of manner as well as courtliness. It arises from a certain habit of will in the soul that is known in its effects and its strong achievements in rejecting vice and imitating virtue. Nobility cannot any more be left to posterity by inheritance or in a testament or by law, than it is left by knowledge or by inclination. Nor because of famous statues of ancestors does nobility dwell in the house of the descendants. Wherever it may be found, nobility is only delighted by purity of mind.

Persuaded by this, Marius, a new man,[9] cleansed the army which the avarice of Metellus, a noble, had infected. He conquered an enemy that had often conquered leaders who were respected and of high rank. He bound in irons a king who had bound the minds of the nobles in gold. What does this mean? It is very clear that these people, like Metellus, were ignoble; but may we not say that those are noble who stand by virtue? For those who wish to possess the truest nobility, not the shadow of it, it is necessary to strive zealously to practice virtue, and to flee, reject, and condemn all kinds of vice.

ABOUT POMPEY THE GREAT

The conqueror of half of Asia ended his life with a single mourner on the shores of Egypt.

Suddenly many people came into my room and surrounded me. First among them stood Flavius Fimbria, disordered both in dress and manner. He complained that, starting as a follower of Marius, he arrived at the height of the Roman consulate; among other acts of bravery, while he was an ambassador to Nicomedia in Asia, he seized the army of the consul Valerius Flaccus and killed him. Everyone then thought that Fimbria should be Imperator of the Army, but Sulla was ordered there and Fimbria was driven into flight at Thyatira. Here he was besieged, and was driven to such desperation that he took his own life in a temple of Aesculapius. With him came Fabius Hadrianus, deploring that

[9] A man whose ancestors had not held high office.

when he went with a band of slaves to take over the kingdom of Africa, the leader of the slaves surrounded his house at Utica with brush and set fire to it, so that he was burned up there with his entire family. A great multitude followed that I willingly ignored; then I saw Pompey. Fortune commanded me to relate the great adversities that befell him after his long spell of good fortune.

Actually the extent of his accomplishments is so great that when I realized what I had to do, it seemed my pen would falter under the enormity of my task. But what of that? I can only work in proportion to my strength; if his life seems longer than the others, I will try to relate it succinctly.

Gnaeus Pompeius, the son of Gnaeus Pompeius, sprung in an illustrious birth from among the most notable families of Rome. As soon as the best qualities of youth appeared, they provided further indication for the future which the luster of his birth had presaged. While still a young man Pompey rallied what was left of his father's army after the latter had been killed by a bolt of lightning.

When the city of Rome was in danger because of the sedition of Marius and Sulla, Pompey joined the party of Sulla. At Regium in Cisalpine Gaul [10] he killed Brutus, one of the leaders of Marius' party, after he had annihilated Brutus' troops. Then in Sicily, which was held by Gnaeus Carbo, another of Marius' captains, Pompey stripped him of his camps and deprived him of most of his army. But Carbo fled Sicily and was arranging a flight to Egypt from Corsica when he was captured and brought back into Sicily. Pompey, obeying Sulla, ordered him killed together with many of his

[10] Reggio, Lombardy.

friends; though Carbo had defended Pompey in his youth and protected his paternal inheritance, Pompey feared the strong power of Sulla more than he respected his own obligations.

Sicily, then, had fallen to Sulla's party, and Pompey, made a member of the Equestrian Order in place of consul, crossed over to Africa, still occupied by leaders allied with Marius. Here after the great successes, near Utica he became the victor against Gnaeus Domitius Ahenobarbus, defeating his troops and killing him during the fight. And when he had conquered all Africa, with the complete agreement of the inhabitants, he took the imposing title of "Great."

Then Sertorius, a man full of guile yet at the same time bold and able, left Africa for Spain, fearing the power of Sulla. There he was made leader of the Lusitanians.[11] Afterward it happened that Sertorius was killed by the treason of his own followers. Metellius Pius then defeated Hyrtuleus, who had taken over the army, and he also captured the important city of Belgida. After Pompey, himself, had overcome Bisania, all Spain came into the power of the Romans.

But as soon as the civil war had quieted down, pirates of Cilicia [12] infested all the Mediterranean Sea and coastline with their plundering and raids. By order of the Senate Pompey organized an expedition against them. He divided the Roman fleet under various captains, and at the same time with speedy foresight occupied all the sanctuaries of the pirates. Then with the ships that he commanded himself he destroyed Cilicia, which had provided the spark for the war. As soon as the pirates were driven to fight, from the first blows of the bows of the ships, the victor was obvious. Pompey,

[11] In Western Spain and Portugal.
[12] On the south coast of Turkey, across from Cyprus.

with the plaudits of all, captured the pirates, who confessed themselves beaten. So within forty days from the
time the expedition was organized, the war came to a
satisfactory conclusion without the loss of any Roman
ship or any Roman blood. By taking the Mediterranean
Sea away from these corsairs, Pompey made it safe for
all men and brought it back again under Roman power.

Then Pompey advanced into the East, and after con-
cluding an alliance with Hyrod, King of Parthia, turned
his arms toward the other powers. He partly destroyed
the power of Mithridates, then later conquered him
completely in a night battle. Traveling through Asia
beyond the limits of Roman control, he reduced everything to ruin. When he learned of the death of Mithridates from a messenger, he brought an end to a war that
had lasted for forty years. He traveled to Syria and
Phoenicia, famous for their vicious fighting. He entered
the city of Jerusalem, captured the famous Temple of
Solomon and went into its secret places. After he had
struck down the chiefs opposing him, he raised Hyr-
canus to Chief Priest and King and conquered his uncle,
Aristobulus, sending him to Rome in chains.

He overcame all nations and their kings between
Mount Caucasus and the Red Sea, so that nothing profit-
able seemed left for him except the heavens. Finally,
when his conquering had come to an end, he had turned
almost half of Asia into a province for the Roman
people. Thus (as he afterward told the Senate in
person) after he had conquered twenty-two kings, he
returned to Rome great in both deed and name. How
much more glory did Hercules or Alexander the Great
achieve with their deeds? In one triumph alone, Pompey
was borne to the Capitol on a chariot drawn by elephants, and in addition, by the decree of the Senate, he
alone was raised to the office of consul for the third

time. And to the many public honors private ones were added also, and he was proud of his famous children by a very distinguished marriage.

However, when Crassus was killed and Caesar was waging war in Gaul, Pompey governed the republic as he wished and was most successful with affairs of state; eventually he refused to obey any authority. Therefore, urged by the enemies of Caesar, he had a law passed by the consuls that no one could carry on business in the Senate while he was away. But Caesar felt that the law had been promulgated against him and that he was defrauded of both the consulate and a triumph. When he heard that the Tribunes of the Plebeians, interceding for him, had been driven from the city, from Ravenna he went into Italy. Pompey, learning of this and anticipating a civil war, had already been made Leader by the Senate. Followed by almost everyone, he went to Capua with the consuls, then to Brundisium, and from there, secretly by night, into Epirus. As if this had been the place fixed for the civil war, he was besieged for a long time by Caesar, who followed him there. But with his legions and auxiliaries he made a breakthrough, and a forced march brought him to Pharsalia, the location of his destruction.

Caesar followed him there, also, and for a little while Fortune stood apart. She showed herself wavering as if in doubt whether to save her Pompey or let him fall. Yet almost all the nobility of Rome and the power of all the Eastern kings stood there favoring the side of Pompey. She compelled Caesar and his troops to plunder the crops and at the same time urged Pompey to battle, which he did not wish at all. From this, the victory of Caesar followed. After a great slaughter both of citizens and of foreigners, Pompey saw that the field was Caesar's, and with a few retainers fled to Larissa, the first evidence of his shame. Here, though offered honors, he enjoined the citizens to save the honors for the victor. Troubled and fearing for his safety, he quickly fled in a boat that he ordered taken to Lesbos where Cornelia, his wife, was living. After a tearful farewell from both his wife and the inhabitants of the capital city, Mytilene, he changed his ship. He gathered together some of the refugees and ordered that the prow of the ship be directed toward Egypt. He passed the shore of Cyprus, expecting the loyalty of Ptolemy, whom Pompey himself had made king when he killed Carbo. But when he saw an evil sign at a large edifice called Cacobasilea, near Paphos, he held his course for Egypt.

Before Pompey came to the shore, the young king, who knew beforehand of both Pompey's arrival and misfortunes, with more profit to himself than loyalty to Pompey, sent a small ship filled with faithful troops to meet him, as if he were about to receive Pompey honorably. The old Pompey, obeying the decree of the fates rather than his own plan, entered the boat leaving his wife and associates behind. He was scarcely aboard when two soldiers, Achilles and Photinus, on orders of the king, drew their swords, and before Pompey could say anything to collect himself or arrange his clothes for an honorable death, they severed his neck. They fixed his head on a lance and carried it as a spectacle for the people through all of Alexandria as if it were evidence of a great victory. Then the king wrapped the head in a cloth and presented it to the victor over Pompey, to obtain his good graces. The body itself was driven back and forth on the waves of the sea all day long as a sight for the barbarians. At night, Codrus, a Roman soldier and quaestor [13] of Pompey's who had fled with

[13] An important elected official who collected and disbursed tax revenue.

him, drew it secretly onto the shore. Nothing else of the
battle was left but this, and after Codrus had gathered
the driftwood that was on the shore, he made a little
fire and placed Pompey on it. With some mourning and
a few tears Codrus buried what was still half-burnt in
the sand.

Perhaps Fortune was ashamed that she had been the
guardian of one who had such greatness of soul, who
had received such bright honors, who had served with
such majesty, and that while she was on his side, he
had been left to the rocks and the fishes. Oh, the tremendous turn of events: the old man killed by a boy;
a Roman killed by a barbarian; superiority killed by
mediocrity; an emperor killed by a servant; one who
gave to life killed by one who received from it. The
lacerated body was made the plaything of the waves,
and at night it was half burned on a small fire then
interred on a beach by a lonely man. If, a little earlier,
he had died in his own country—what funeral pomp,
what lamentations by all the consuls, Senators, and
citizens; what a procession of all the patriarchs of the
state bearing him away! How many military insignia,
tokens of power and triumph left for his bier? How
many lauds chanted, how many eulogies? How piously
the ashes would have been collected. All this homage
sought in his lifetime was lost in his miserable death,
and he was covered by a small mound on the Egyptian
shore.

Why are we dolorous mortals so proud? Why do we
seek riches by our labors? Why do we put our faith in
what is about to perish? If such a great man fell, why
do we think nothing can happen to us? We should have
sympathy for Pompey, but we should fear for ourselves
even more, and most zealously we should seek after
what is humble, lest, if raised up, we would always be

in the grip of fear and at length come to our destiny in anguish.

A FEW WORDS OF THE AUTHOR'S

I would like to be still, and with a certain right, and to put down my pen after having related both the lofty rise and melancholy fall of these leaders, especially that of Pompey the Great. What more can be said about the unstable power of Fortune? I do not believe that any mortal ever fell from so high a pinnacle. But since it is granted that we may continue our history to our own times, it does not seem to us that today they are any less exalted nor less subject to the commands of Fortune. By the kind permission of the readers I will follow my plan, and if the great person you are expecting does not materialize, still the lesser figures can, with delight, bring great profit.

A HUGE WRANGLING MULTITUDE

The stories of all those destroyed by Julius Caesar were put aside for that of a very great orator.

I had just finished lamenting the fate of Pompey the Great when a long column of grievers arrived. They were rulers and other notables, both from Germany and from Gaul, who had been deprived of their greatness, their titles, and their lands by Julius Caesar. Those who had fallen in the conflict at Pharsalia were present, as well as others, almost too numerous, who had been butchered or destroyed wherever the plague of civil war had struck. With them came Ptolemy, an unhappy young man. He complained bitterly about his scheme against Pompey, his war against Caesar, and his death on the Nile delta. Then Juba, the very mournful King of Lybia followed him. By his pride and his disdain he prevented Scipio [14] from donning the purple as he did himself, but he was sad that he had joined the party of Pompey and he condemned himself. But now he worried about this in vain, because he had already been defeated by Caesar, deserted by his followers, and expelled from his own kingdom. He was brought so low that he made an agreement with Petreius. They would run one against the other with their naked swords and thus each bring about the other's death. But when he killed Petreius and was himself unharmed, he was completely deranged. He begged a servant to cut his throat.

After him followed Aristobulus, the King of Judea, who complained that he had been unjustly deprived of his throne by Pompey, and with his children had been sent as a prisoner to Rome. He escaped, but was re-captured. Finally when Pompey was killed he was given his freedom by Caesar, and Aristobulus hoped he would be given back his kingdom too. With his soul bursting, he and his confederates were on their way toward achieving his desire, when for the third time he was intercepted by the leaders of Pompey's party. Now he was poisoned.

Scipio showed up querulous because the slaughter in Africa had deprived him of all his hopes. He was made successor to his son-in-law, and in a ship was to go to Spain. Tossed about by many storms, he was carried to Hippo, where he was surrounded by the fleet of Publius Siccius, one of Caesar's followers. Here he found death by his own hand rather than test the clemency of

[14] The grandson of the Scipio who defeated Hannibal.

Caesar. Gnaeus Pompeius, the son of Pompey the Great, was there, complaining. He was grumbling not so much that after his defeat by Caesar at Munda he had been caught hiding in a cave, and killed, and that his head had been presented to Caesar at Hispalis [15] then given to the people; he complained rather that his death had followed too closely on that of his father to fulfill his vow to be avenged on the treacherous Egyptians. Then Brutus and Cassius bemoaned both their murder of Caesar and their defeat at Philippi.

There was Trebonius mourning not only his condemnation for Caesar's murder, but also the fact that he, himself, had been cruelly slaughtered by Cornelius Dolobella at Smyrna. Here, too, was Decimus Brutus, who had been involved in the same conspiracy. He was wailing that after his military debacle he had been captured and beheaded by the Sequani.[16] And Basilicus, a Roman nobleman, well known among the assassins, grumbled that he had been slaughtered at the hands of his own servants. And there was Gaius Toranus, one of the praetorian magistrates, a dolorous man. He was afraid of nothing within his own home, but fell victim to an attack by soldiers. On his heels Dolobella himself was whining that, after beating Cassius many times before in battle, he was in turn beaten by him, and reduced to such an extreme that he took his own life.

Many others were cursing their fortunes and groaning about their various fates. Among them that very brilliant and eloquent orator, Marcus Tullius Cicero, entered in silence, his head lowered. I put all the others from my mind and gazed at him in admiration. I wanted very much to relate the glory of this great Roman and his unworthy death. But as I thought about this prince of

[15] Both of these cities are in Spain, the latter now Seville.
[16] River dwellers in Northern Italy and Southern Germany.

Latin eloquence I held back, knowing that my abilities
were too weak for such an undertaking. He, and no
other, was worthy of writing about himself. However,
so that one who should bask in the light would not be
left in the shade, I began to chide myself:

"Come on! Prod your soul! Jostle your spirit! Renew
your strength! Show what you can do, and do what you
can for a very worthy cause. For no one is so stupid not
to know that clouds cannot obscure the rays of the sun.
Your writing is unskilled, thin, and without style. But
what of that? If opposites placed next to one another
shine more brilliantly, at least, if nothing else, he will
make your dull embellishments appear more glittering
by the wonderful beauty of his graces. If you offer praise
less complete at least you will give the opportunity to
those who are more learned to supply them. Perhaps he
will instill in you something of his secret from the very
place it now abides, and you will perform better than
you think."

Spurred by these arguments, though I am not equal to
it, oh, most excellent of orators, star of Latin eloquence,
by your leave will I not write about you and your destiny just as ordered by Fortune?

ABOUT MARCUS TULLIUS CICERO

*The greatest orator of them all was killed by a man he
had earlier saved from the executioner.*

A resplendant star shining forever both over the city
of Rome and over the world, Marcus Tullius Cicero was
born in Arpinum, confirming all that has been said about
that city. He was a member of a family famous for the
ancient kings of the Volces, and while still a boy,

showed the heart of a man. As if he thought his native hamlet too small for the breadth of his future or as if a high tower could send its light further into the world, Cicero left Arpinum and went to Rome. There the filth of lust was spreading, as well as the love of avarice, and the vice of ambition; and these excesses were setting the souls of men on fire.

As much for his understanding of affairs as for the strength of his character, he was received by the best and most aristocratic Romans, and earned both the rights of citizenship and the highest honors. By his residence a new citizen, but the oldest by the love the Romans bore him, he rose continuously until with Caius Antonius he reached the high office of consul. By his efforts the city which ruled the world was saved from conflagration, ruin, and slavery. The terrible spark of Lucius Cataline's nefarious gang, threatening the ruin of the city, burned hidden within its heart. Cataline considered more the social position of his ancestors than his own character, and in order to widen the scope of his vanity, he had very often sought public office but always without success. This angered him against the republic, and he gathered around him some young noblemen and girls. Lieutenants selected from these wild conspirators by their designs promised a dark future for the name of Rome.

God prevented their dire conspiracy from taking place. Quintus Curio revealed his whole plot to his attractive wife Fulvia, whom he loved very much, and from her many others learned about it, among them Cicero. Cicero kept the Senate and his associates in the dark concerning it, but with marvelous adroitness he uncovered all the plans of the conspirators. He did not say anything in public until he discoveerd what had been going on and knew all their plans accurately, without any possibility of contradiction. But he checked their first efforts by placing obstacles wherever they wanted to break out their sedition. During the time of his consulate Cicero did not hesitate to accuse this rebel frequently in the Senate, though Cataline was upheld in the elections.

He revealed Cataline's preparations by making public the names of his associates, by showing what he had done and was about to do. Cicero's pointed orations did not fail to prick the lassitude of the Senate as well as the perfidy of the conspirators. As a result Cataline left the city for Faesulae. On the plains of Pistoria he gathered troops together and clashed with Antony, the consul, who had followed him with another army. Cataline's soldiers were cut to pieces by the disciplined troops of Antony. In this fight Cataline himself was wounded and killed, and his efforts at rebellion produced only a bloody victory for Antony. As for the other conspirators, Lentulus, Cethegus, and Sabinus, they were captured in Rome on the advice and efforts of Cato. At night in the Tullian dungeon they were killed by executioners who broke their necks with a noose. Thus the security of the city, which had been threatened, was restored, and in this way also, Cicero, in a toga, overcame rebels in arms.

The doctor who cures an invisible malignancy within his patient is preferred to one who takes his skill and ointments to a wound large and easily observed. So our Tullius was renowned widely by this one exploit, deservedly called the outstanding protector of Rome. This was enough to ensure his fame, yet he acquired a glory that was to endure longer than the one he acquired more easily. Cicero, it seems to me, was sent here from God and already possessed genius from Heaven, yet working with continuous diligence he became so eloquent that he surpassed Plotinus Gallus of Cybelia, the first man to teach Latin rhetoric at Rome. And he surpassed Milta-cilius Plotus, one of the Gracci, Hortensius, and all the most eloquent orators both Greek and Latin, taking over their reputation.

As if this honor were not remarkable enough, he still desired to enter the holy portals of philosophy. To the approval of all, with his rich oratory he defended first Quintus, then Roscius against Chrysogonus. Afterward he went to Athens where he searched carefully into what ancient and contemporary philosophers had dis-covered concerning the outward manifestations and most profound truths of nature. Among the Athenians he at-tracted such admiration by his eloquence that they be-lieved he excelled not only Pisistratus and Pericles who, by the skill of his florid oratory, had forced the free Athenians to put their necks under the yoke of defeat, but also Aeschylus and Demosthenes. Cicero's skill also surpassed the honeyed skill of Plato, to whom while still a child sleeping, the satisfied bees brought not Hyblean nectar but actually Castalian.[17]

Initiated into the revered teachings of philosophy and honored by the praises of the Greeks, Cicero returned to Rome and defended Aulus Licinius, Archias, Milo, Gnaeus Plautius, and many others, favorably impressing all who heard him. He reconciled Deiotarus, King of Galatia, Marcus Marcellus, and Quintus Ligarius to Julius Caesar, who had previously mistrusted them.

What more can I say? By his eloquence Cicero was able to change a person's mind to whatever he wished, no matter how obstinate the person might be. Whatever is left of his orations is not enough to demonstrate his

[17] Hybla was a mountain in Sicily covered with flowers and noted for its honey. Castalia was a fountain on Parnassus and thus Castalian honey is a metaphor for eloquence.

power, for even in what remains, the best part of
Tullius has been lost. They can be read, but they cannot
be heard.

His wealth, his honorable marriage, his beloved children, his remarkable friendships, his clients, and other
such gifts of Fortune that overflowed on him I have
saved until last, but so no one thinks I confuse these
insignificant gifts, however much they appear to contrib-
ute to happiness, with his honors that were as great as
they were apparent, let me relate his downfall, one
unworthy of him. Granted that the renown of this
famous man was tremendous, still it was not secure.
Whenever a man's position is shaken, the sign of his
future ruin is clear. Because of certain envy Cicero endured exile for a year in a house at Atina that he received from Gnaeus Plautius. Then, in a dream, he
received a warning that everyone wanted him to return
to Rome, and there he was received by the Senators
with the greatest enthusiasm. In the quarrel between
Caesar and Pompey Cicero followed the leadership of
Pompey, and for a second time had to leave the country;
for after Pompey's faction was broken up, he was exiled
again with almost all the Senate. He was recalled a
second time, not because anyone asked for it but because of Caesar's victory. Subsequently disgraced for his
conspiracy in the murder of Caesar, he fled alone to
Formianum.[18]

Affairs at Rome progresed along various lines. Cicero
was condemned by Mark Antony, one of the triumvirate against whom he had once inveighed too freely.
Caius Popilius Laenas received the order for Cicero's
execution from Antony and with terrible ingratitude pursued Cicero. Not long before, Popilius had been freed

[18] Now Gaeta, on the coast north of Naples.

from a capital charge because of Cicero's moving oratory. Popilius attacked the man to whom he owed his life and forced Cicero to bend his neck to the sword. Like a savage he struck off the head that had saved his own. Not content with this impious deed, he cut off Cicero's right hand. As if he had performed a deed bringing the greatest honor and help to the state, he bore the head and hand to Rome. Here treachery waxed strong, and the grim relics were fixed to the Rostra.

Oh, dear Heavenly Father, where is your righteous anger? Where is your destructive fire, that flash of lightning? Where will you open up the earth? Why did you not send this accursed man, this ungrateful beast, down to the lost souls at the moment of his enormous crime and in the sight of the miserable Romans? Why, I ask you?

While we are instructed by Cicero's unfortunate end that we should have no confidence in worldly distinctions, the vacillating Plebeians of Rome were rebuked and shamed by this horrible crime. When in the Rostra they saw the head of the man who had prevented theirs from rolling in the gutters of the streets, they were moved to compassion.

AGAINST THE DETRACTORS OF RHETORIC

The divine origins of rhetoric and why the skill should be strenuously cultivated.

Certain foolish and roaring men, braying rather than speaking, sometimes permitted themselves to fall into a detestable madness. Where they can, they steal the weapons from the hands of rhetoric and use these weapons against her. They are not afraid to open their filthy mouths poisoning everyone, proclaiming that rhetoric serves the purpose of deception rather than that of need, that any kind of words are sufficient to express an idea. Very foolishly they try to condemn both the labor we employ in rhetoric and the beauty that results.

This can be answered. It happens they say more than enough to turn their strong poison against them, if I wished to waste my efforts against such a demented group of men. But I do not struggle against such vanity. Their folly is too well known, and I think to conquer such people I need only shake my spear in the empty air; but for the help of others, it will not be superfluous, perhaps, to say something.

Animals show their feelings by a movement of their heads, by a whistle or a roar, but to man alone was it granted to express thoughts in words. Nor was this without cause; for how could nature in any other way more wisely separate mankind, endowed with a divine soul, from the beasts, controlled only by sensuality. Servants of their senses, the thoughts of the latter are only on earthly things, and they take pleasure only in these. For the beast it seems superfluous to have a tongue for easy speech. We conclude, and rightly, that unintelligent beings had far better exist without tongues.

But the origin of man was truly from Heaven; he was created for the purpose of reflecting upon things celestial and was given speech not only as a necessity but as an enhancement. By this means we communicate our most profound reflections on higher things, on changes in the elements, on the advancement of various matters, and on our perception of iniquities. We join with other men in intelligent understanding. We praise virtues; we deprecate vices; we receive and transmit the results of

teaching. In short, we reveal whatever the mind experiences through reason, and we comprehend the significance of what we learn.

As rational beings we pray to God, and by the con-
fession of our deficiency we venerate Him. Therefore
there are two sources of our speech: first, what we learn
from our nurse. This is, by its nature, unrefined, outside
of us, yet common to all people. Then a few of us receive from learning, a source enhanced and polished
according to our diligence, and one which is favorable to
our development.

Who is so lacking in good sense that he would not
prefer something artistically produced to something
which is not? And this holds especially true when ar-
tistry is added to something great already. Is not the
man senseless and foolish who would disapprove when
someone undertakes the effort to cleanse his writing of
whatever crudeness he finds there and beautifies it with
graceful elegance? We are not always asking a servant
to prepare our food, nor speaking only to a rustic about
farming. It is frequently necessary to ask God for something that we need and to give thanks for what we have
received. It is not becoming to reveal the spirit of our
thoughts to the Creator of all things in a disorganized
way, or to sing His praise in words that are not melo-
dious. Besides, if someone has said that God regards
attitude of mind rather than beauty of prayer, I will not
trouble to contradict him.

There are still many other forces, however, which,
unless they are controlled by oratory, might develop
from insignificance into the greatest calamity to mankind. If we do not possess the skill in oratorical com-
position appropriate to the occasion: words not rough
or sharp, but now calm and placid, now agreeably discerning, now containing beautiful figures of speech, now

serious wisdom, and—in addition to these embellishments—a public delivery suitable to the immediate need,
then we would not be able to restrain ordinary men lost
in the passion of anger (let alone a king). How would
we be able to console or cheer someone who is dejected
or melancholy, how inspire someone slothful and torpid,
how restore to frugality someone given to laziness and
waste? Really, I do not see how. I recall sometimes
seeing persons indifferent and unskilled in speaking, try
to cool the anger of others. They only fanned the anger
into a deadly conflagration. They brought tears back
into eyes that had already been dry; the energetic they
drove to timidity and sloth; while they tried to make
excuses for themselves, they actually accused themselves.

Therefore, so we do not fall into errors we wish to
avoid, and instead attain what we wish, we must work
with the greatest attention and skill to perfect our
speech. While there is no necessity which drives us to
this end, duty should compel us. To avoid the storms
of winter or the heat of the sun, we do not make the
walls and roofs of our houses out of grass or reed. On
the contrary, we construct them of stone and hewed fir
and decorate them with pictures. We cover our bodies
according to our ability with the richest garments, gayly
decorated with gold and gems, though we might be
protected against the sharpness of storms and the breath
of the wind by a simple cloth, woven by a crude hand.
We drink out of goblets decorated with gems, and we
make other things which appeal more to the eyes than
to any other part of our body. Why, therefore, do we
neglect eloquence, by the cultivation of which we delight our ears and at the same time gratify our intellect?
So certain moderate sounds of stringed instruments
bring their delights into the minds. At first they seem
with their sweetness to lead the mind into relaxation;

then from all sides the sound finally collects everything into itself.

In the same way well-polished speech flows into the mind by way of the ears, and it first soothes the mind by its brilliance. Then after it has driven away all other ideas, this skill so draws its audience to it that if you observe the audience, you will see that they are transfixed and unable to move, and that they all agree with the ideas of the speaker.

But enough on this subject for the present. The idle chatterers, and those whom a less liberal nature has granted little skill, gnash their teeth against those who have been trained, and they bemoan their ignorance. Or, acknowledging their own inferiority, they vex themselves without bettering themselves. As long as they remain obstinate and continue to prefer trifling subjects in discourse, they will find themselves overcome by the truth.

A NUMBER OF MOURNERS

The author is visited by two of the Triumvirate and some of their victims.

I thought I would end this particular book when I had related the stories of those who had already appeared to me, for I began with the commander-in-chief born at Arpinum and ended with the prince of eloquence born in the same place. But I was set upon by a crowd of clamoring people, and was unable to do so. I turned my attention to them and saw Sextus, another son of Pompey the Great, tearfully approaching. I knew that he had been born and raised with the greatest promise because of the triumphs and extensive fame of his father. But he was seized in the cruel storm of life, which drove him to piracy among the very pirates his father had defeated. Pompey had brightened the city with his victories, but his son darkened it with disgrace and violence, provoked it with war and famine. With a shaking voice he confessed that after the death of his father he had suffered numerous misfortunes. He combined armed convicts with great numbers of troops from Pompey's army, but at the hands of Octavius Augustus was conquered in a naval battle between the Sicilian cities of Mylae and Naulochus, and was put to flight. When in Greece he tried to renew the war, but was conquered again and captured by the leaders of Antony's party. After a short while they killed him.

Marcus Lepidus, a member of the Triumvirate, appeared. He was illustrious not only because he had been commander of cavalry under the dictator Caesar, but also because by his efforts he had established harmony between Octavian and Antony, and with them had assumed the duties of the third member of the Triumvirate that had ruled the world. But when Africa was given to him he was carried away with the power of his twenty legions, and his arrogance opened the path to his ruin. When he turned his arms against Octavian, he was not only conquered and deprived of his power, but was deprived even of the insignia of his command. Dressed in dark robes according to the custom of a suppliant, he begged for his life and his family properties. He agreed to be exiled permanently by Caesar Augustus and to live quietly as a private citizen.

In the crowd was Lucius Caesar, exiled by Antony, his nephew, and Lucius Paulus, by Lepidus, his brother. And with them were many others whom Fortune had thrown from the greatest heights to disgrace and misery. Among them all it seemed that Mark Antony, the Triumvir, could best carry on the plan I had begun. He appeared with Cleopatra, but now his aspect was changed.

ABOUT MARK ANTONY,
THE TRIUMVIR
AND CLEOPATRA, QUEEN OF EGYPT

Antony could have ruled the world but chose instead love on the Nile.

Mark Antony was a nephew of Julius Caesar by his sister. Cruelty, passion, and ruthlessness carried him to the very loftiest summit of power. When Caesar was killed by the conspirators, he was found to be the first among the heirs; but Octavian had taken the order of the heirs unto himself and was left the name of Caesar. Incited to fury by his wife Fulvia, Antony immediately took up arms against his co-inheritor. He was then adjudged an enemy by the Senate. He attacked Decius Brutus and besieged him at Mutina, for the consuls, Hircius and Pansa, and with them Octavian, led an army against him, and he lost his army and fled. After Lucius Antonius was defeated by hunger at Perusia,[19] Antony achieved not the ruin that he deserved but rather success. By the efforts of Marcus Lepidus he was reconciled to Octavian, and all three of them together, under the name of the Triumvirate, took over the state. And so that Octavian's faith in Antony would be more firm, Octavian's sister, Octavia, married Antony. Then Brutus and Cassius were defeated at Philippi, more because of

[19] Modern Modena and Perugia; the hunger was the result of Octavian's siege of Perugia.

the good fortune of Octavian than by the strength of
Antony, and it seemed that the power of all Asia was
left vacant for them. Octavian returned to Italy; Antony
fought in the East. There, by the efforts of Ventidius,
the might of the Parthians was almost destroyed, and
they made a treaty with the king by which Syria was
given them. Inspired by vanity, Antony deposed Hyr-
canus, and proclaimed Herod, son of Antipater, King
of Judea.

Fortune was now invited to make way for his downfall; for suddenly, and contrary to the treaty he had
made, Antony and his legions invaded Parthia. But with
barbarous cunning the Parthians attacked him unexpectedly. They caught two legions by surprise and destroyed them with arrows. Upon suffering this disaster,
Antony was advised by someone that on the next night
he should take flight with the rest of the troops through
the steep mountains and the passes. Part of this group
was cut down by the enemy who followed them; others
died of hunger and thirst; many became prisoners, and
not a few died in the snows of Cappadocia or in the
heat of Armenia. Although he had left with sixteen
legions, he arrived at Antioch with scarcely five.

According to some, Antony was now seized by the
beauty of the lascivious Egyptian, Cleopatra. Under the
spell of her attraction, he was feverish and ran around
as if he were about to put in her lap all the titles he
had received for his victories and the rewards of his
triumphs. Impatient for her love, he vowed that he
would come to her; and in order to achieve this desire
more quickly, he seized (by treachery) Artabanus, King
of Armenia, once the son of Tygranis, then ordered that
his huge treasure be given into the hands of this avaricious woman, with the king and his son bound on a
silver chain. By this opulent gift Antony had appeased

his shame and flight from the Parthians and earned
Cleopatra's embraces. He laid down his arms as if all
the prestige of Roman honor rested with her charms
and gave himself over to indolence and sloth. He wasted
his time in never-ending sensuality and gluttony, and
allowed himself to be captured by stupidity. He ordered
it proclaimed that he had divorced Octavia and married
Cleopatra.

Actually Cleopatra was descended through many
kings from King Ptolemy, son of Lagis, and, according
to the will of her father, she succeeded to the Kingdom
of Egypt with her brother, whom she married. Finally
poison raised her above her husband, but she was
robbed of the kingdom when a younger brother was
made king by Pompey. Cleopatra remained guarded in
a prison at Pelusium until Julius Caesar arrived victorious at Alexandria. After Cleopatra had eluded her
guards she went to see him, and captured him with her
extraordinary beauty. They became lovers. Then her
brother was drowned in the sea and she gained sole
primacy in the kingdom. Finally she was first mistress,
then wife, to Antony. Her sister, Arsinoë, had fled into
the Temple of Diana at Ephesus, and she had Antony
kill her there. She attempted to seduce Herod so that
through him she might appropriate the Kingdom of
Judea for herself, and she was so insatiable for gold
that she impiously destroyed many temples of the gods.
Finally—and this was most detestable—she coveted
power in Rome. Arising from a banquet in which they
both had been engrossed, she enticed Antony now with
flattery, now with enticements, now with warm embraces; she asked him what we would not deny her, and
by the judgment of Lucius Plantius, she was victorious.
Antony believed that the Romans and the Italians were
weaker than the Parthians, and promised her what she

had asked in copious nocturnal pleadings. Nor was there any delay. After he had gathered together a force of Eastern kings, he took up arms against Caesar Augustus. A fleet was prepared which you would have thought carried the perfumes of Saba, Arabia, Syria, and other countries as well as the robes and pomp of kings, rather than the arms of conflict.

The force of the winds and the sea led the fleet as far as Actium. Augustus opposed it and came to the island of Leucadia at the base of Mount Leucatea in the harbor of Ambracia.[20] Here at this time Antony's forces were thin, partly because of a battle on land and partly because of lack of provisions. For this reason he was finally tempted by Fortune to a naval battle. But after a long fight the end of Antony's foolish pride now approached. The Egyptians began to turn their ships about. Their leader was the famous Cleopatra, the woman who had begged and wished for the Roman Empire, the woman with golden ships and purple sails. And immediately, Antony, her proud sponsor, lowered his ensign and followed her. So by sail and oar, and caring more for their preservation than for world power, they went to Alexandria where they began to rebuild the army. But the troops of Octavian and his subordinate generals were victorious. Octavian followed the Egyptian fleet and achieved the surrender of their forts and towns, then threw a siege around Alexandria. Soon everyone in the city was imperiled by hunger, and ultimately Antony sought conditions for peace but was not able to obtain any. He then went into a royal mausoleum where he took his own life with a sword. Cleopatra surrendered, and with the charm of her eyes and figure, she tried in vain to lure the young Octavian into desiring her. When

[20] An island in the Ionian sea.

she heard that she was to be held for a triumph, she eluded her guards, and went to the place where Antony lay, anointed with perfumes and decorated with all her royal insignia. She bared her breasts, and after placing serpents next to them, she lay down to die. As if in a quiet sleep her spirit was released. But Octavian thought that her life was still struggling to survive and ordered Psillis to suck from the body the strongest poisons that were there. But in vain he tried to revive her. So that their living should be completed where it began, he ordered Antony and Cleopatra to be buried in that sepulcher. Thus this intelligent man, while he had ideas worthy of him, still hoped for the greatest reward from Fortune. Unhappily he caused his own ruin through his imprudence. Neither was Cleopatra content with what Fortune had offered her. Her body, softened with the greatest delicacies, used to the most tender embraces. was at last embraced by serpents while she was still sensitive to sight and touch. And the poison nourished the same blood that had been nourished by wines. The beauty she displayed with her feminine vanity, she buried alive, tricked by the volatile barb of Fortune. And she who had yearned for great power, finished her life in a mausoleum.

A QUARREL BETWEEN TIBERIUS, GAIUS CALIGULA, AND VALERIA MESSALINA

Messalina defended her profligacy against two of the greatest profligates.

From among those who surrounded me, complaining, a spectacular and revolting quarrel assailed my ears, and I directed my mind and eyes toward the quarrelers. The altercation was caused by Tiberius Claudius Nero and Gaius Caligula, both dolorous in their dress as well as in appearance. Yet when they saw Messalina among the mourners, they began to rail viciously and harshly against her. First Caligula spoke:

"Messalina, you repulsive champion of lusting, do you come here to see Aemilia Lepida weeping, Livia Medullina sobbing, the languishing Plautia Herculanilla, or Aelia Paetina rejected? [1] The temperate and aged Claudius, ruler of the world, granted your desires before everything else. Perhaps you came here to see Drusus, who was strangled by Pirus (both your stepsons), and Claudia, exposed before her mother's doorstep so that you might derive some enjoyment out of your mean hate for them. Or did you come to find again some sleeping potion, poppy seeds, or medicinal leaf, by means of which Claudius was sunk, not only in sleep, but almost in death while you were busy with your orgies?"

Immediately Tiberius contradicted him:

[1] The first two were betrothed to Claudius, the latter two married to him before Messalina.

"Not at all! For she knew that this famous guzzler, though he was teetering, due to the kindnesses of Agrippina, had already joined the heavenly banquet, and with Jupiter was emptying those beakers overflowing with ambrosial nectar. Actually Messalina's fierce desire so aroused her that very often in a single night she offered herself for adulteries without number. At the end of the night, more exhausted by her physical effort than satisfied by the pleasure, she foresook her whoring cells in borrowed clothes. By the gods, I think these really were brothels. Because many people came to these orgies, she went there often to meet with her debauchees. But you did not understand, Messalina; these were occasions for melancholy, not for delight."

To these accusations Messalina replied, sincere in her speech, her expression determined:

"Against such slanderers, how do you think a woman can be lured to speak? I knew that place very well, who came there, and the reason even if you had been quiet about it. I suffered a grievous fall of my fortune. Though I was born of an illustrious father, Valerius Messalla Barbatus, and enjoyed the marriage-bed of an emperor, I died a shameful death in everlasting infamy. I was weeping copiously then I saw and heard you, mournful also, and I think your death was no more elevated than mine. Now I am less melancholy, and I will restrain my tears for a little while to answer your accusations.

"I am ashamed; I will not deny it. I was lascivious, licentious, and an adultress. And I always enjoyed the company of many men. Although I was sinful, still I was not without some excuse. I remember—and am happy to remember—when Messalla, my father, asked a mathematician about my birth. He answered:

" 'This child was born to you, Messala, when the sign of Gemini, children of Latona, in conflict with Scorpio, rose in our hemisphere following Mercury, regarded as the enemy of Orion. Venus was joined to her Mars, and to the open head of the Dragon in the eastern sky. A change of the sky took Jupiter into the sign of Pisces, the fish, and the unhappy old man, Ganymede, into a very deep night.'

"Thus it seemed that all the signs of the sky were met in the power of love, and under the influence of this sky I was born to this compulsion. Although it was an abominable sin, still it was part of my nature. Anyone would wish sincerely with all the power of his soul to be able to overcome this weakness. Hercules will excuse the fact that a woman failed. Although he was given shoulders that would support the sky, still he never was able to conquer the power of love, for Hercules was conquered by the same force as I was.

"Truly if Scipio Africanus or Marcus Cato had reproached me as you did, or if I had been Sulpicia, the wife of Fulvius Flaccus, or the ancient Lucretia, then I would have been quiet, and you would have reproved me justly. But why, I pray you, do you vituperate the descendants of the gods? So that I can refute both of you attackers at the same time, I wish you senseless juveniles and unworthy children of your just father, Germanicus, would recall that you are the most noted of those who were drawn by your damnable lust and ardor toward your own sisters Agrippina, Drusilla, and Livilla —but especially toward Drusilla. It is no secret what you did, often even by force, to the most honorable married women even in the presence of their husbands, whom you betrayers had invited to your houses.

"I presented doped wine to the besotten Claudius so that I could put him to sleep. But you gathered poisons from everywhere so that you could get rid of the whole human race. I put Claudius to sleep so that I could

have greater freedom for my passions. You wanted all
the citizens of Rome to have a single head so you would
be able to satisfy your cruelty with a single blow. When
you look at your own behavior, you ought not to attack
wretched me so insolently and heedlessly. Really, Gaius,
you should rid yourself of shame before you accuse
others. But I will take this up with you at another time.
Now I will turn all my force against this awfully dirty
old man here.

"I wish you would tell me, Oh, most brilliant Tiberius, you who have attacked my improprieties with so
much careful verbiage, if you recall that island in Campania, Capreae, where you chose a secret retreat for
your pleasures, or rather, that you built as a workshop
for your obscenities. You tireless preacher against the
passions of women. Didn't you arrange the filth of your
perverted obscenities there After picking up from everywhere male and female whores, or anyone who had
invented some novel sexual practice, weren't you then
able to accomplish your plans? You avidly stared at
these ugly performances so that your own worn-out
person could recover its virility; then those obscenities
would continue with your participation. Isn't it true, you
horribly filthy antique, that you, not worthy to be a
member of the human race, as the lone inhabitant of
the island, had all the woods, caves, and remote hide-
aways prepared with theaters and lodges and fixed up
so they catered to your incestuous appetite? And then
you filled them with women and young boys so everywhere you went you could watch what went on or
engage in it, if you had the strength. What do you accuse me of, now? When I was young and easily aroused,
at night I would go to a bordello dressed in someone
else's clothes. You, openly, all day long, when you were

old and inert, lived in those whores' cells. Why didn't you look carefully at yourself, you miserable creature, before reproaching me for my adulteries? You spoke against yourself when you thought you were attacking me.

"But if, perhaps, you wish to refute these insults by asserting that chastity is the only treasure of the honorable woman, which, once lost, she tries in vain to recover. This does not apply to men, nor does a man suffer any dishonor from doing what has caused many a woman to become infamous. I would have much to blame you with if I wished to speak at greater length. I don't believe that anyone can ignore all virtue unreasonably without disgrace. But if it is true what they say about you, then you aren't evil for the things I mentioned; you performed the greatest and almost unparalleled treachery.

"Let me put aside your ill-spent youth, Tiberius, your laziness and your imbibing, for which you were called Biberius Caldius Mero, a drinker of warm wine. If you would look around you, you would see Agrippina, your daughter-in-law, weeping and in misery because of your atrocities. You were not ashamed to accuse this innocent girl of trying to flee your poisoning, first to sanctuary by the statue of Augustus, then to the army abroad. Because of this you exiled her to Pandataria.[2] There you still had her beaten by a centurion so that she lost an eye, and she tried to escape your cruelties and horrors by starving herself to death. You were fearful that the shortness of her life would shorten your tortures, and you attempted to push food through her throat by force, trying in vain to keep her soul, destined to leave her

[2] Now Vandotena Island, roughly off Naples; used by the Romans as a prison.

body. But she knew you could take away the life of
many who didn't want to die but could not give life to a
single person who wished to die.

"In the midst of my own miseries I had compassion
on Nero [3] and on Drusus, the children of Germanicus
and the brothers of this horrible young man here, whom
I see behind you moaning over what happened to him.
They said you were envious of the prayers of people
for the health of Nero and Drusus. First you insulted
them in various ways, and then in letters perfidiously
accused them in the Senate. By these means they were
judged enemies of the state. Finally your cruelty brought
you to this. Nero was banished to the island of Pontia
and died there of hunger. Drusus, it is reported, in the
lowest dungeon of the palace, was terrified when the
executioner showed him a halter and a hook.[4] He killed
himself finally. Although he had cried loudly for hunger,
he was denied any food, and you gave him instead the
stuffings of a mattress to eat. For others, their hatred for
Drusus and Nero abated with their deaths. But you, as
a climax, ordered their remains scattered around, so that
no one was able to collect the dead to put them in a
tomb.

"You throw those mushrooms and drinks I gave my
husband up to me as if I were ignorant of your villanies,
you veteran of evil days. Tell me, I beg you, who doubts
that on your orders Gnaeus Piso, then ruler in Syria,
poisoned your brother, a very distinguished leader in
battle, as useful to the Plebeians as to the nobles of
the state? And Drusus, too, whose body you followed in
such humility. I deceived my husband with a cup. You

[3] Not the famous emperor but an uncle. Nero was a common
name in the Claudian family.
[4] The hook was fastened to condemned prisoners to take them
to the Tiber.

deceived your brothers with poison. I toyed with the weak. You killed the most skilled of your time.

"You low pest, you ought to be execrated with the most deadly of words. Brother was fierce against brother. Before they were born, they were one and the same blood, one father, one mother, raised in the same house, cared for by the same parents, obeying the same discipline and custom. And as their life began so did their friendship. Wild beasts, not born in the same womb but joined only by the same hope, save one another from injury by a stranger. And men, to whom reason is given are not ashamed to practice violence against their brothers and to embitter their souls.

"But I come back to you. If I wanted to relate all your savagery, there would not be words enough. Let Sejanus rise up and tell his story. After you had his statues pulled down, you ordered him executed, then put on a hook and dragged to the Tiber.

"It is enough for me to have replied to you with these few words. I know that you are iniquitous in your soul, I in my body; you in your thoughts, I in my actions. Your acts were harmful to all the human race, mine to no one (except for the shame I put on womanly chastity). I was executed by the order of a ruler; you among pimps and whores, in wretched brothels, exhausted in limp old age, avid for sex, but impotent in the attempt. Why do you rebuke a woman? You accuse me of lust, a vice common to everyone. But what a spear I have punctured you with, you depraved, murderous, old man!

"Now let me turn to this insolent juvenile. Where now, I beseech you, Gaius, is your foolish evil and empty glory? You, a mortal, dared pretend that you were a god and allowed temples to be erected, statues raised, victims presented and sacrificed, prayers offered, your name invoked, and had yourself worshiped by your enemies.

You castigated my incontinence among your miserable followers. Oh, you gorgeous face, crawling down from the altars, from the dwelling place of the gods into the midst of swords where you were rightly massacred and then thrown into the world of the unfortunates to bark at Messalina. I think that Castor and Pollux, among whom you lived, ejected you out of their ancient propetry as a newcomer. I believe that Jupiter Capitolinus was not able to bear your ever increasing ignorance, reproving his power. Who of the gods, I pray, Mercury, Mars, or Minerva, has driven you out of his hearing? By the gods, it was unjust, after you had filled his head with all your ideas. You came back for the good of the state. To exalt forever the honor of your name, you ordered soldiers to kill your brother, Nero, when he was off guard. You did the same to his father-in-law, Silanus, to Ptolemy, son of King Juba and grandson to Mark Antony, to many of the Senators, to the consuls and the praetorian guard, and even to the common people of Rome on whom, after you had locked up the granaries, you inflicted the hunger of Erysichthon, who was punished by Ceres with such hunger that he devoured himself.

"Oh, most splendorous father of fathers! In you we see fathers who act with too much love toward their children, for they kill them with sure starvation rather than preserve them for an uncertain fortune. Was this the advice of Jupiter and Queen Juno? I think this was rather the idea of Mother Venus in order to capture the deep love of your subjects. I venture that she did this so that you might set upon the Senate against their wishes, and they could see the sufferings of their children when you threw both innocent and guilty to the beasts for the good of the state in your own time. She also taught you, as a sign of your talents and as special evidence of your

clemency, to write those notable little poems, one entitled, 'The Sword' and the other, 'By the Dagger.'[5]
These my husband Claudius discovered after your death.

"But the gods, toward whom you were contemptuous
in your madness, rewarded the innocence of the others
rather than the prayers that you addressed to them, and
allowed you to die easily. You do not really seem to
have been punished enough for your evil. Endure the
torment that you deserve, most miserable of beasts, and
teach yourself first to suffer for your own crimes before
you snarl at others."

I had listened to these retorts with the greatest eagerness and found them far from tedious. The cruel men
were very unsettled, and acknowledged her victory in
silence. Covering up their heads, both of them prepared
to go away. Then far away there came into view the
one who won his laurels among the harpists, that monster of the universe, Nero Claudius Caesar. Never before
had a wild beast like him appeared. As if by the memory
of his atrocities, he silenced the others. One so great had
fallen, and his collapse was such that I will write about
him very earnestly, for the importance of the task I have
taken up deserved it.

ABOUT NERO CLAUDIUS CAESAR

*The most infamous Roman emperor combined cruelty,
perversion, histrionics, and poetry.*

At Rome the Ahenobarbus family was descended from
the Domitius family of whom Lucius Domitius Ahenobarbus was the founder. After many generations of great

---

[5] They were actually lists of persons to be killed.

offices, famous triumphs, and brilliant marriages, the family gave birth to Nero Claudius Caesar, whose parents were Lucius Domitius and Agrippina, the sister of Gaius Caligula. The astuteness of his mother combined with the kindness of Fortune to enable him to achieve great heights. When he was a child of three, he lost his father by dropsy, and his mother was sent into exile by Caligula. After Nero had been defrauded of a third of the inheritance that was left him, Fortune maintained him rather poorly under two teachers at the home of Lepida, his paternal aunt. Then during the reign of Claudius, Agrippina was recalled, and Nero was much advanced because of the memory of his grandfather, Germanicus, as I surmise.

Messalina wished to kill him, for he was now regarded as an equal of Brittanicus; [6] actually Claudius, disgusted with her adulteries, ordered Messalina killed. Too, Claudius had fallen in love with Agrippina because of her charms, and was forced by the Senate to marry her, though it was hardly according to law.

Not long after, when Nero was eleven years old, he was adopted as a son by Claudius, as a result of his mother's efforts, and was recommended to his friend, Seneca, a very famous man, and one especially learned. As a young man he was married to Octavia, a daughter of Claudius and Messalina. It was not long after that, by Agrippina's machinations, as some writers believe, that Claudius was poisoned with mushrooms, of which he was very fond. While his death was a secret, Nero, seventeen years old, took power, disregarding the claims of Britannicus. At the beginning of his reign he gained much goodwill by his praiseworthy deeds and gave promise that he would show himself the greatest of rulers.

[6] His uncle and her son.

So from a boy who was poor, from a youth deprived of his inheritance, he rose to the summit of the world and ruled other kings. To his sovereignty he even added some brilliance, for in his youth he had studied almost all the liberal arts with remarkable intelligence. His facile skill led him through the disciplines of oratory and revealed to him the most sacred lessons of philosophy. By the judgment of certain writers the arts of oratory were revealed to him by Seneca, and Nero's skill came only from him. Agrippina, however, took him away from the study of philosophy, believing, with feminine logic, that philosophy was not proper to a ruler. Nero gave himself so thoroughly to the study of poetry that, if he had continued as he had begun, he would have been very famous, according to many persons' judgment. He never gave up poetry to the extent that he did not compose lyrics easily and profusely. He also wrote a poem against Clodius Pollio, the praetor, entitled, "Luscio." Nero was outstanding in painting and sculpture, excellent in music, in voice as well as lute and pipes. He was very skillfull in driving horses and chariot. He was strong of body, and in any kind of contest, daring, vigorous, and hardy.

He was very desirous of an eternal name and put great expense into building, for he believed that there was fame in walls rather than in virtue. At Rome he built a house of wondrous magnitude, occupying three miles. He first named it "The Passageway," and when it was destroyed by fire, he rebuilt it more expensively. Then, instead of The Passageway, he called it "The Golden." Within it he placed not only shrubbery, but lawns, vineyards, fields, and woods as well as a lake of enormous size. He filled this area with almost every kind of animal, both domestic and wild, and fish in great numbers. The roof he decorated with gold fretwork, the halls and chambers he equipped with tables of ebony, gold, and the most precious stones and pearls marvelously constructed. He added other extraordinary innovations, but these were more for license than for beauty. At Baia, in the vicinity of Misenum, where he found the surroundings enjoyable, he had a huge lake constructed. For it he brought water in abundance from the Sarnus River, a distance of six miles, through an aqueduct of baked stone, pillars, and forty arches. In addition he had mountains dug out and built underground tunnels for a navigable waterway so that he was able to go from Lake Avernus all the way to Ostia.

And there were many other constructions also, but why should I lengthen this description of his talents and great buildings? I do not believe any one so evilly abused his good fortune as did Nero, for as will be very clear, the discernment that nature granted to him was crushed by the grossness of his body. If a man does not have a stable mind, we are easily deceived by what he does; and I suggest that no one was so perverted who for such a long time led his life in contrary directions. To be sure, after he had taken up his diversions and constructed other buildings, for a short time he corrected some of the habits of the citizens and made some very useful laws. He granted to both the common people and to the nobles the greatest gifts as if he wished to strengthen his power by these earthly things.

But gradually he fell into an astonishing and indescribable wantonness. He laid aside the dignity of imperial rank, and without any embarrassment, as if he were accomplishing something advantageous to the state, he both sang in public and competed on the harp against Greek and Egyptian performers. What is even more dishonorable, very often among prostitutes, hawkers, and debauchers he demonstrated how skillfully he could perform. He often drove his chariot, and while the Roman people watched, he performed the pantomime "Hero," and would enter into the scene just like one of the actors. When he won the prize, starting something new, he entered the city in triumph, as if he had returned from the Sarmatia.[7]

He spent his nights like his days, running in and out of taverns, brothels, and whatever scurrilous places there were, not without danger to himself and injury to those who were with him. He extended these diversions until he lost all restraint and began to do them openly. He precipitated himself into gluttony and lust; he spent his days in banqueting and continued until late at night in perpetual gorging. As he traveled by boat between Baia and Ostia, he ordered taverns and banquet-halls filled with food and drink built everywhere along the shores. There were also houses for noblewomen. As he went by, Nero ordered those who appealed to him to invite him inside. It has been ascertained that he lewdly diverted himself with these women, who had previously been free of such disgrace. As wives he had first Octavia, then Poppaea Sabina, and finally Statilia Messalina, but he continually took advantage of virgins for his companions, as well as innocent youth and brides. He was not even ashamed to take by force a Vestal Virgin, Rubria, for his own enjoyment. What is most infamous and perhaps incomprehensible, is that he was seized by a fatuous love for a certain Sporus. Insanely he tried to change the boy's nature into that of a woman by removing his testicles. When this proved useless, he dressed the boy like an empress and went through a festive nuptial ceremony with him. On another occasion in Greece, he went through a marriage with a freedman, Doryphorus,

[7] Poland and Western Russia, with the connotation of being very distant.

and on the first night Doryphorus emitted cries and groans like a virgin whose chastity is being violated.

But why do I relate incidents that are so repulsive? What cannot be imagined about him whose reputation was so lurid and well known that people believed he had an affair even with his own mother? These depraved acts have overshadowed his waste. Habitually he fished with nets of gold and purple lines. He never wore clothes twice and played dice at forty sestertii a throw. The mules drawing his vehicles or bearing his litters he shod with silver shoes. He wasted many other things profusely in a combination of avarice and atrocity. In addition to other actions both infamous and filthy, in sacrilege he robbed the temples of their statues of gold and silver and other ornaments both within the city and without. Finally, when he had made it known that in Rome the ugliness and age of the buildings as well as the circuitousness of the streets were offensive to him, he allowed the whole city to burn up in order to rebuild it again more beautifully and strongly. For six days and seven nights no one dared to save his goods, and from the Mecenatian Tower Nero watched in great delight, singing of the capture of Ilium. When the fire was over, he allowed no one to gather up what was left of his goods. He stood beside those who searched the ruins and collected for his treasury what was sprinkled among the ashes. How many temples of the gods; how many venerable buildings decorated by the victories over the Latins, Carthaginians, Macedonians, Asiatics, and Gauls; how many public theaters, how many statues of the ancients were destroyed and obliterated?

What more can be said? His cruelty became so inflamed that no one anywhere, not by night nor even with guards, was safe against him. Among the damnable crimes he committed was this: he had Britannicus, his

brother, the son of Claudius, killed with a poison con-
cocted by Locusta,[8] not, as some writers think, because
he feared that Britannicus would take power on the
memory of his father, but actually because Nero envied
his singing voice that seemed more pleasant according
to the judgment of those who heard it.

At the beginning of his rule, Nero had entrusted to
his mother almost all the affairs of state. However,
neither the power she gave him to acquire the Empire,
nor their incestuous relationship, nor the bonds of
family spared her when she reproved him too sharply
about his disreputable activities. First he deprived her
of all the honor of her position. Then he expelled her
from the palace at night without possessions of any
sort, and ordered that no one should receive her. But
he was still possessed by fear that she whose efforts gave
him the throne would depose him. An attempt to poison
her was frustrated, as was the use of a machine he
contrived to take her life. Finally he gave the appearance
of being reconciled to her, and called her from Rome
first to Puteoli then to Baia to celebrate the festival
of Minerva. But he ordered that the ship to be given
her be so flimsy that it would be capsized by the waves.
Not far from Bauli the ship fell apart, but Agrippina
was carried by the tide to a small villa. Here Nero
ordered a decurion sent to kill her, and went there to
see that she was dead. He was not only able to observe
the crime that he committed without tears, but eagerly
touched parts of the dead body with his hands. Some
parts of her body he praised and some deprecated to
his friends who were with him. And because he came
thirsty into this disgusting assemblage, he drank with
hands still bloody in the presence of the corpse.

[8] A famous poisoner mentioned in Suetonius, Tacitus, and
Juvenal.

He had many others killed. For no reason at all he commanded Seneca, that very eloquent old man and his teacher, to have his veins slashed and take poison. Among his victims there were also Senators and many nobles of the city whom he had assassinated for a variety of reasons. After his constant massacres, he proceeded to other enormous horrors. Under the spell of certain evil-dealing necromancers and their followers, Nero put to an unworthy death Simon Peter and Paul of Tarsus, these very saintly persons, teachers, and princes of holy religion.

Because the Romans ignored the degradations of Nero for so long, their downfall now began in the provinces. By many nations they were held in contempt and hatred. The Britains removed themselves from Roman power. The Armenians, after a great slaughter of Roman allies, sent the Roman legions under the yoke and then organized themselves under their own law. The Gauls under Junius, their governor, defected, and finally the Spanish, under Galba, revolted. Although these events occurred far and wide, still Nero did not cease his habitual lascivious activities. When he was attacked by the Senate in various censures, this man, who before had menaced all the world, now began to know fear. He pretended to gather an enormous expedition together to be sent into Gaul and Spain, but he did nothing except talk and immediately fell back into his old ways. The Romans were indignant, but, as it always had been, they lacked the courage to speak the truth in his presence. In secret they attached satiric verses and other insults to his statues and pictures. Then they began to relate openly many horrible stories against him, saying on the street corners that it was true what Domitius, his father, said on the day Nero was born. When his friends congratulated him, Domitius said that nothing so detestable or evil to the people could have been born to him and Agrippina.

These events made it clear enough to Nero how feelings had turned against him. Because of this as well as dreams and signs, an overwhelming fright engulfed him, and anxiously he thought about death. Locusta gave him a poison, and afterward he put it in a golden jar to save it. He was unsettled by various worries, thinking now to flee to the Parthians, now to seek help from Galba, now to call the Senate and the Roman people together at the Rostra to ask their pardon for his past. When he was distracted by these anxious doubts, he put off any resolution until the next day and put himself into a profound sleep. His former disgraceful habits still had such power over him that with his affairs in such a dubious condition, he still dared to sleep. But once, when he awoke around midnight, he saw that the soldiers who guarded his room were away, and he called for some of his personal friends from among his slaves. They neither came when they were called nor did anyone return who was sent after them, and Nero pounded on the doors in vain for a few of his followers. When he went back to his room, he discovered that the jar containing the poison had gone, and so had all the furnishings. In a frenzy he turned to each one of those who were still with him and offered his neck, begging them to cut it. But no one wanted to do it, and he complained that he had neither friend nor enemy. He was fearful and longed for calm. Offering Phaon, his slave, freedom, he went to his house on the outskirts of Rome, as the night turned into day. His feet were bare, he was covered only with a tunic, his head and face were hidden by a scarf. He got on his horse accompanied by four men. Making his way along the Via Salaria and Via Nomentana, he heard many things said against him by those who were passing by.

He arrived at his destination, and after he sent off his horse, spread his clothes under his feet to make his way through the thicket. He stopped not far from the villa. So he could enter secretly, he got down on all fours and made his way through a narrow tunnel into one of the small rooms. Then, to escape the feelings of the Romans, he ordered a pit made the size of his body, and tearfully began to prepare for the needs of burial. He learned that he had been declared an enemy of the state by the Senate, and that he was being sought for execution. He called vainly on those who were with him that if some of them would show the way to a voluntary death, he would be induced to do the same. He now heard the din of those who were searching for him, and finally fell on his own dagger. When he had collapsed and his spirit had almost left him, a centurion came up who tried in vain to check the blood flowing from the wound with his cloak. When Nero asked him what he wanted, the centurion said he was to take him back to the throne, and he promised to help Nero. To this Nero only replied, "You are too late, but here is true fidelity." And with these words his blackened soul, like his blood, left his body. Amidst the wild joy of all the Romans, he was buried with little ceremony at the monument of the Domitian family by Ecloge and Alexandria, his old nurses, and by Acte, his mistress.

SOME AFFLICTED CELEBRITIES

After I had completed these few words about the degradation of Nero, more people in distress made their presence known to me. Among them, very mournful, was Eleazar, the Israelite. Once he had been the leader of thieves and murderers, but he had been sent to Rome by Felix, the Procurator of Judea, and there he was crucified. Then Servius Galba came, bloody from the garden of the Argives. Tearfully he told all about his noble ancestry, his insignia of rank, his famous marriages, his happy accomplishments, and his ascent to the highest office in Rome. Then he cursed the instability of Fortune by whose efforts he was killed. Gregarius, a soldier, bore his head to his enemy, Otho, who gave it to a group of servants and lackeys. Finally it was redeemed by Patrobius, one of Nero's freedmen. This Patrobius ordered it thrown on the funeral pyre, thinking in this way to insult the memory of Nero.

A young man, Piso Licinianus, followed Galba sadly. He had been adopted as Galba's son, and from this high position was dragged blamelessly to a most severe death. Salvius Otho complained, though in moderation, that just as he had become emperor by the death of Galba, he was overthrown by his own legions and the envoys of Vitellius. He despaired, and relinquishing the heights of so great a dominion, he plunged his sword into his body with his own hand.

Next to him was Vitellius himself, still besotten with wine. It happened that he gave up his life and the state in even greater degradation than the others, and it seemed that I ought to add his story to the others.

ABOUT AULUS VITELLIUS CAESAR

This emperor was interested more in feasting than in ruling and tried to sell his throne to his enemies.

Some authorities said that Vitellius was descended from Picus, son of the Faun King, grandson of Saturn, and the nymph Vitellia. There are others who maintain that he came from an ancient shoemaker of Luceria (a city of Apulia), who lived at Rome. The most prominent descendant was Publius Vitellius, a member of the Equestrian Order in Rome and an administrator for Octavius Caesar. Lucius Vitellius and all his brothers were born of Publius, and from Lucius came Aulus Vitellius. It is believed that this last Vitellius had been in charge of male prostitutes for Tiberius, and on the island of Capreae he led those disgusting boys and youths who were known by the name of the "Sphrintria." His handsomeness and figure provided the step toward his first advancement. After the death of the shameless Tiberius, Vitellius' skill in driving a chariot attracted the good graces of Caligula, and his skill at dice the friendship of Claudius; too, he was in accord with the debased customs of Nero. All these activities obtained for him the greatest honors and a priesthood that he desired.

However, it is uncertain whether he was either too free in his expenses and his lasciviousness, or entirely too moderate in his profits (I believe that this was least important for so detestable a youth), or so restrained by his great need that he scarcely was able to get enough money by enforced gifts from the foreign provinces. This, however, is sure, that when Galba was emperor, Vitellius hoped to go into Lower Germany to meet the army, but lacked money for the journey. He took a pearl from one of his mother's ears, and after he had given it to a moneylender, he had the money. Although this was a small sum of money, it opened a path to the heights that everyone thought appeared closed to him. The army, aroused against the emperor, received him, rather unexpectedly, with particular friendship, and this gave him hope for the ultimate power. He had no gifts, so he established his friendship with the army by his indulgence in filth. Before a month had passed soldiers seized him in the room where he was accustomed to dress. They saluted him as emperor to the joyous approval of all, and as a sign of sovereignty he held out a sword known to have once belonged to the divine Julius Caesar, which he had picked up at the Temple of Mars.

Vitellius joined an army from Upper Germany with his own, and upon learning of the death of Galba divided the army into several parts to move against Otho, who had taken the name of emperor. Then Vitellius learned that Otho had been repeatedly defeated by Vitellius' subordinates and had taken his own life; so Vitellius, decorated with the insignia of triumph, went through the cities and entered Rome dressed in a military cloak, his sword at his side and surrounded by a troop of armed cavalry to enhance his glory. He took the office of Consul permanently, and, ignoring the ancient religion, assumed the office of the chief priest on the very day of the defeat on the Allia, a day always abhorred by the Romans.[9]

What more could a mortal man expect then? From a male prostitute of Tiberius, he rose to be emperor in

[9] The anniversary of a defeat by the Gauls, 390 B.C.

the capital of the world; from a charioteer he rose to become a celebrator of triumphs; from a dice thrower with depraved addictions he became the chief of priests. Thus, from the depths he achieved the heights, as if in the rise to the summit virtue had no place, diligence no value.

He ruined himself with the same corruptions that he had practiced up till now, and also found greater ones. He turned to indolence as if that were the most worthy way of life. He gave himself over to gormandizing and finally to complete gluttony. And when his own sumptuous feasting, carousing, and revelries did not suffice him, he left these for the homes of others. Even in the midst of sacrifices engaged in religious duties at the altars, he grabbed food still not prepared. From restaurants he ordered half-eaten foods prepared the day before brought to him. Dressed in his robes as chief of priests, apparently possessed of the insatiable hunger of a wild beast, he devoured what had been cut into filets and placed on the altar for worship. And he filled his obese stomach with voluminous drink. Then drooping with wine, he staggered around the altars with a faltering gait.

What more can be added? Vitellius had so weakened himself with this fatuous vice that he easily became inclined to all sorts of evil. Little by little, among other infamous sins, cruelty entered his consciousness. Not long before, he had pardoned, too indulgently and without thought, those who harmed him. Now he assaulted the innocent, delighted in the torture of others, and even arranged the deaths of his relatives.

In the eighth month of his reign his northern armies, the Moesian and the Pannonian [10] and the eastern

---

[10] Now Bulgaria, Yugoslavia and Hungary.

armies, the Judeans and Syrians, suddenly revolted and swore allegiance to Vespasian. Vespasian prepared war against him, so Vitellius sent his brother with a fleet, and a conflict took place at Bedriacum. Vitellius learned that part of these forces had rebelled, and that another part of both the land and naval forces were defeated. Broken in spirit, he made a disgraceful pact with Flavius Sabinus, the brother of Vespasian. He promised that if an agreed sum of money were given him, he would freely give up his sovereignty. It is my belief that affairs prevented him from eating as he wished any longer. Quickly, and for a little money, he promised that he would throw aside the cares of the public, then with his customarily stuffed gullet, would glow brighter than the stars.

But this was not enough for him. In mourning, he ascended the Rostra and tearfully swore to the people assembled there that he wished to put aside the burdens of rule. If he had been consistent in his plan, perhaps he would have been able to banquet to satiety again, but in reality he was a weak man. He was inspired to hold on to power by the frivolous clamoring of the people and the soldiers. Puffed up by this light breeze of the crowd, he sent German troops against Sabinus and his rebellious associates. He had Sabinus slaughtered and set fire to the Capitol where he burned up the others.

Vacillating, however, he now went back to his original plan to resign, and in the presence of many city officials offered them the sword that he had earlier taken instead of a scepter. When none of them would take it, he declared that he would put it in the Temple of Concord, but some of them idiotically persuaded him that he, himself, was concord, so he kept it. But what will I say? His spirit told him what had happened and what was

to come, and he believed he had strength for nothing
more. It is hardly credible that a man accustomed to
feasting, who preferred the odious quiet of restaurant
and tavern to the noise of battle, could in abstinence
occupy himself with the business of the largest empire.
So he strongly urged the Senate to allow him both
peace from his enemies and time for deliberation. But
before he received the answer, he heard that his enemies
were already close by. He could not resist the fear that
separation from feasting would kill him, so he ordered
a meal and ate in abundance. When he finished, he
went secretly to the Aventine Hill with his baker and
cook, in order to take flight toward Campania. But then
he heard a rumor that there was going to be peace. In
this vain hope, he whirled around in the middle of his
flight and returned to the palace. Here he discovered
that affairs were still unsettled and that his enemies
would break in. Unhappy and distressed, he took a belt
full of gold, and all alone went to the door-keeper's
room. To seclude himself, he barred the door and in
front of it tied a dog. Then he set a bed and a couch
against the door so that it would not yield easily to
any force used against it.

But the palace had been taken over by advance
units who were searching for him everywhere. Unrec-
ognized, he almost escaped them with his deception,
but he was finally recognized, and he pleaded in vain
against being put in prison and chains. With his hands
at his back and a noose around his neck, he was led
half-clothed into the Forum. Everyone in the street
mocked and scorned him in the most disreputable terms,
and he was the target of all the dirt, filth, and dung
along the way to the Gemonian Stairs, which led to the
Tiber.[11]

[11] The regular route of condemned prisoners.

By this time his brother and his son had been butchered by a thousand wounds. Vitellius was handed over to an executioner and, with nothing to alleviate the pain, was slowly cut to pieces with the greatest torture and in view of all the people. A hook was fixed in his nose by an official; with everyone screaming insults against him, his decimated corpse, like that of a malodorous dog, was dragged to the river and tossed into the depths. So Vitellius' life, his drunkenness, and his power all came to an end.

AGAINST GLUTTONY AND GOURMANDS

The author proves that moderation in diet leads to physical and moral well-being.

To be sure, gluttony is an abominable vice, and—like lust, sloth, and avarice—should be avoided; and wrath and blind fury must, as well, be condemned. Gluttony is bestial and deadly. In gluttony we use immoderately what nature has given us for our sustenance, and to avoid the vice, we should not readily slacken the reins of temperance in our appetite. Nature, uncomplicated, is content with moderation, and rejects what is prepared with human cunning. The present age, the Saturnine age of gold, gives shameful testimony of this. To alleviate their hunger and thirst, most ancient people relate that for them acorns and brook-water sufficed. Diogenes, in more recent times, approved this repast with the addition of wild greens and roots. And much more famous, the Most Glorious One, He who was sanctified in the womb, was nourished on locusts and honey in the wilderness. In place of this diet our younger and wanton age not only discovered the flesh of harmless animals and wine, but in addition substituted artificiality instead of letting nature provide. It is now considered wise to incite the calm appetite by introducing spice or mulling wine with outside flavors. Would that the discovery of these things had been enough to satisfy us! But much that was gluttonous went beyond this to an extreme, without mentioning those vices that excessive gormandizing allowed or how many diseases it introduced into the troubled body. But while we do not plan to enumerate all these, still we do not wish to pass over them in silence.

When the voracious glutton sits down at a loaded table, devouring now this, now that, and greedily draining the overflowing mug, he does not do this to satisfy the wants of nature, but to stuff the chasm of his corpulent belly, warmed with the strong vapors of steaming platters. Instantly, from ecstasy he goes into frenzy, and imagines he has achieved greatness. An immense ostentation follows; then an easy credulousness, the revelation of secrets, the miserable deprecation of whatever occurs. Ears now respond to flattery, the heart to any kind of confidence, and the mind rejects nothing except what is worthwhile. The brain, stupefied, suffers with dizziness; there is frequent gaping, forgetfulness, indecent talk, conflict of the senses, a floundering step. Finally there is repulsive belching and vomiting, because what he devoured and what the gullet forced down into it, the stomach did not have the strength to support.

Sometimes, in contrast, the stomach retains all the food. The gourmand very painfully begins putrefying, and by this putrefaction of the blood the body's whole organization of nature is brought out of balance. This results in the disfiguration of the eyes and the mouth as well as in tremors, paralysis, staggers, stammering, dropsy, consumption, gout, a feverish itching, filthy scabs, a violent fever, and nausea, for the stomach refuses all food. In addition to these, very often even an untimely death results. Verifying what the most learned doctors have told us, more people have died from banquets than from battles.

Most of these gluttons will, therefore, be seen among the drowsy, the delirious, the diseased, those dying shamefully, the slaves of their stomachs. The glutton is constantly arranging meals. Inspired by his oversized goblets, he thinks he can get out of any kind of work.

Oh, too degrading a life! How satisfying it would be— if the acorns of the ancients are too sparse—to follow the moderation of the men of history. With moderation, the vices are indeed suppressed and the virtues maintained, and the minds of men easily raised to higher things. The whole strength of the body is conserved for the best habits. When Vitellius on the royal throne spurned these, his satiety did not take away disgrace from his person nor pain from his body.

THE RENOWNED
FRANCIS PETRARCH AND HIS
REPROOF OF THE AUTHOR

*Petrarch chides the author on his sloth and
explains the meaning of true fame to him.*

It has frequently been observed that too much repose
is the mother of dullness and the enemy of creativity,
and I have often proved that observation by my own
sloth. Not long ago, however, I fell into almost a trance,
for I had let myself go in the most complete laziness;
desirous of slipping away, I let my memory take flight.
I was plunged into a deep sleep, unable to move, and
seemed almost dead. Though frightened, I was sometimes revived by my anxiety for the work I had under-
taken. Overcome by lethargy, however, I lay down and
said:

"Fool, why do you torture yourself with such a job
as this? Why do you harass yourself with such continuous labor, pouring over the tomes of the ancients,
when no one is driving you? Do you yearn to extend
both your days and your name by a reputation acquired
in scribbling anew about the ruin of the men in history?
Oh, what an empty desire! The hour will come, and
is here now, which will take you away from the things
of this world. It will destroy your fragile body. It will
turn you to ashes. I pray you, when you will no longer
experience things of the moment, even if the tongues of
all the earth will sing the praises of no other name but
yours, what honors and pleasure will be left to you then?

202

When the physical form by which you are known has been lost, everything transitory has really been lost to you. I venture that it is uncertain whether your name, which you are trying to glorify to those who come after you, will be commonly known to many others, or even whether it is now. If it is now or will be in the future, you work for others as much as for yourself when you could be resting lazily. Therefore stop, and what remains of your life, pass according to the demands of the occasion."

I was therefore half (if not completely) conquered by sloth, arguing about these and many other ideas, and lay down on my couch. But suddenly it seemed to me that I saw a man standing in front of me, sent from where I do not know. He was unassuming in appearance and demeanor, with a handsome and cheerful face, a pale complexion. He was wearing a crown of laurel, was wrapped in a regal cloak, and obviously deserved the highest respect. When I had fully opened my eyes and had completely shaken off sleep, I looked at him intently, and recognized him to be Francis Petrarch, my great and venerable teacher, whose counsels always spurred me toward virtue, and whom I had admired above all others from my earliest youth.

After he had regarded me for a little while with a penetrating expression, he began speaking:

"Why are you lying down, oh, famous Professor of Lassitude? Why are you stupefied by the false arguments of inertia?" I blushed profusely and dropped my eyes, cursing what I had said to myself just a little before. To escape the reproof of this famous man, I waited in silence. He continued:

"Have I so obscured your reason by my teaching that you propound the idea of work by commending slothful indolence? Absolutely not! Let no one prefer the sound of words to the profit of work. Why then are you lying down? Have you forgotten that man was born to work? You have begun your journey, and now that you have almost reached the end of it, you stop, turned aside by a fatuous opinion. So you are not deceived by this banality, pay attention to what I have to say.

"The renown that you condemned a little while back is actually a benefit, greatly desired by all men. While it is sought in different ways, it is acquired only through virtue. Therefore, if someone condemns renown, he must necessarily condemn the practice of virtue. Moreover, since we have entered the world, we recognize that light is more esteemed than darkness, and renown is granted to us by a divine gift; the reputation of our deserts is borne on the light even to the ends of the earth. With the greatest luster renown leads the spirit of those who merit it up to the heavens, as if they were on a paved highway. Renown makes very long our too brief span of mortal life, and as if she gave us another life, she bears witness to the honors earned by one who is dead. It is by this means that we praise and honor Moses, Aristotle, Virgil, Scipio Africanus, the Catos, and others, as if they were actually present. We feel a great pleasure within our souls for the renown that they receive from us, for we believe by our labors we will be able to earn the same thing from those who come after us. And thus, in hope, we anticipate a future glory. What man esteems this as insignificant, for surely his body is not enough for him?

"Therefore renown must not be passed over, nor stifled by idleness, nor yet abominated as something vain and superfluous; but by the reason of God's will, you must seek after it with all your strength. And when you try to increase the glory of God, you know that this increases your own as well. You acted foolishly

when you wrapped yourself in idleness, for your name
is or will be (which is quite possible) known to many
people. What, I pray you, is more contrary to charity,
than to be envious of the happiness of others?

"Why do you attempt by laziness to take away what
perhaps God, by your work, wishes to offer to others?
Is it not better to work for others than to waste yourself
away in misery? I wish there were many today who have
a name like yours, yet they could not take what is not
theirs. Others before you have had the same problem,
if nothing was known about them by name. In the
same way your physical appearance and that of other
people are recognized. It is possible to attribute the
deserts of others to your name or yours to others in
the judgment of those who are to come. You should
fear exceedingly lest, while you live honorably, the
disgraces of other persons are imputed to your name.
Therefore, let me say in truth, the virtuous should seek
a hiding place, for I only see the light of the sun
through the smoke from the fire of the elements. Fame
has been good to persons in the past, such as those
who were hunchbacked, lame, or had any kind of de-
formity you wish to name. Fame described them to
posterity as handsome, illustrious, and revered. And this
is your idea of all these.

"If you can, add something brilliant to your soul for
your reputation. Thus it happened with Scipios, the
first Africanus; Cato the Censor; Cincinnatus; Plato;
Aristotle; Homer; and Virgil. If we note something
unworthy, by inventing in our mind we add something
of esteem to them. But if all trace of a person is lost
among mankind, his memory is not lost to God for whose
glory he worked. God observes accurately and cannot
be deceived. And what is most desirable, He rewards
with the gifts that will not perish. And what can one

who works more joyously achieve than to see those talents committed to him by God returned doubly?

"Therefore he must perform, he must work, and he must urge his skill on with all his strength, so that he will be separated from the common herd, and just as those who came before us were of use to us, so will we be of advantage to those who come after. Then our name will be written among the immortals; then we will have eternal fame; then we will believe that in the worldly campaign, we will have fought on God's side, not on the side of sin.

"What more can I add? I would have been able to, and you deserve it, if I had spoken more sharply against your sloth. However, too much severity sometimes breaks the lazy person, rather than refreshes him, and I think that it is best by far to use mildness, so that I may inspire shame for your slothfulness rather than ill will in your spirit. Though angry, I will not drive you with whips. But rid yourself of gloom, and sluggishness; rise up energetically and finish the task that you began. Even if neither glory nor reward come to you from it, you should wish rather to stand guard with an empty stomach than, stuffed, stagnate in lethargy."

So the most famous man of our time spoke to an ordinary mortal. Truly I remember no one who more redeemed his time on earth with continual exertion. By the very strong proof of his life, I am plunged down into the depths, and by no means would I dare raise my eyes to him. Mournful and unhappy, I condemned my foolish ideas, lowered my head and wished that, by his courteousness, he had called different ideas into my troubled breast. Then as if he knew my state of mind, and after the cloud of righteous indignation had fled from his illustrious face, he relaxed his sparkling eyes into a smile and said:

"That you seem to be dejected is proof that you have been purged of your sloth. This is enough—really more than enough. Get up and do not despair because of me. And for the rest of your time, beware lest you are drawn into damnable sloth by eloquence."

I was assuaged by the charm of his words, and after I had been somewhat revived in strength, and though not all the shame had vanished, I raised my face toward Heaven to observe my merciful teacher. But since he had discharged his duty he had gone away as unexpectedly as he had come. Because of his visitation, I had pulled myself together, and by this means God had awakened me from my foolishness. After I had condemned my ridiculous ideas, once more I took up my dutiful pen.

ABOUT ZENOBIA, QUEEN OF PALMYRA

Both a beautiful woman and a great soldier, Zenobia challenged the might of the Roman Empire.

Immediately a troop of Roman caesars arrived, both great in their majesty and overwhelming in their grief. How could I describe all the most sorrowful of them? It would be, in truth, a very long task, and Zenobia, the Queen of Palmyra, bemoaning that she had adorned the triumph of Aurelian, separated herself from the group. So I began her tale.

Zenobia, who traced her ancestors from the Ptolemaic kings, was a woman outstanding in eloquence, charm, judgment, bodily strength, and learned in the arts of war. Because of the extraordinary deeds of her ancestors she inherited a great empire, and she deservedly enlarged it. She married Odaenathus, a prince of Palmyra, and by him had two children. It happened that Valerian was seized by the Persians, and from him Odaenathus immediately occupied the kingdom of the East and took the rank of King with his wife, Zenobia, as Queen, and with his son Herod. After he had gathered an army together, he led it against the Persians to avenge Valerian, whom his sluggish son had neglected. Odaenathus brought Mesopotamia and many other places under his power, and all the disturbances of the Eastern Kingdom he controlled with great diligence and facility; because of this, it appeared the brilliance of Zenobia increased.

Odaenathus and his son, Herod, were ruling with equal rank when they were killed by Meonius, a maternal cousin, seething with a burning envy. His lust and depravity aroused the hate of the people, who, by a true judgment of God, killed him. Zenobia was endowed with the spirit of a man. After the death of her husband and her stepchild, she defeated her enemy and introduced her two small sons, Hermianus and Thimolaus, into the stream of affairs. In their names she ruled the empire for the first time. The two small boys she dressed with the insignia of Roman emperors, letting them go before her in military convocations. These she zealously celebrated through many years, arming herself not according to feminine weakness, but in the glitter of military severity. She demonstrated a vigorous leadership of the armies, occupied the Eastern Roman Empire and held complete power there.

Now, after the Roman leaders had overthrown the tyrants with the death of Claudius Augustus, the government fell into the hands of the Emperor Aurelian. He thought it unbecoming that part of the Roman

Empire should be held by a woman, and therefore turned the army against Zenobia. She, however, was not terrified, but assembled her troops with resolution and marched out in battle formation. But why does this interest us? Although there may be great virtue in one who is rising in fortune, yet he must fall eventually. And neither could Zenobia escape this truth. While she was fighting with her soldiers, she conducted herself as a strong leader; but as Fortune would have it, she was conquered and led captive to Aurelian. Much as he gloried in his many victories, he took special delight in Zenobia. Since she had put aside the characteristics of a woman for those of a man, he did not hesitate to lead her ceremoniously in triumph; she was forced to march in front of his chariot and gave added luster to him. She was a woman of battle and beautiful; she was loaded with gems and had gold bands on her feet. Though she had been conquered, she still exhibited great strength, and, struggling under the load, she was sometimes forced to rest. To the spectators, men and women alike, this seemed correct, even if monstrous. Once a queen, then shown as a famous captive, she finally spent the rest of her life in private among Roman women.

How life, too little considered, is torn apart by frequent and discordant changes! Before, this woman had shaken the kings of Persia and Syria. Now she was disdained in private; before, she was admired by emperors; now she received sympathy from ordinary people; helmeted, she had inspired soldiers; aproned, she heard the trifles of servant girls. Before, this queen, enthroned, had carried the scepter of the East; now she carried pots and pans at Rome.

What more can I say? She proclaimed herself the companion of warriors like Semiramis and Dido before her. If it had been possible, Fortune would have destroyed the name of Zenobia. Therefore, go, unmindful of your mortality; climb high! Either you will respect the winds of Fortune, or, while you are unwatchful, you will ignore their force and will fall to a sure death.

ABOUT ODOACER, THE RUTHENIAN KING OF ITALY

The first barbarian King of Italy easily won his throne and just as easily lost it again.

What person, I pray, could in a little space describe all those I saw around me who had seized the Kingdom of Italy, those who were raised up and then overthrown through their own fault or that of someone else? Therefore it sufficed to choose Odoacer, the Ruthenian,[1] from the group and speak of him in more detail.

Odoacer, then, was of the Ruthenian nation, but I do not have the information whether he was a nobleman among them. Actually he was by nature keen, with a strong physique, and very interested in acquiring booty. He learned that the emperors had left Rome to live on the shore of the Euxine Sea and that Italy was disturbed by the banishment and restoration of rulers and by various other changes. He thought that he could occupy the country as many others had done and assembled a huge and puissant force of Herulians, Thuringians, and Scythians, whom he had aroused with the idea of the spoils they might take. He entered Italy at the border of Pannonia, and after he had crossed the Noric Alps, Orestes, a Roman nobleman who alone knew of the

[1] Later Aquitaine.

arrival, fled with his army as far as Ticinum.[2] Here the Roman army was besieged, attacked, and driven to Placentia, where Orestes met a melancholy death.

Odoacer made his way carving out the road to Rome with his sword and pushing everything aside with his force. When he entered the city, no one resisted him. Augustulus, the son of Orestes, had assumed the purple robe of sovereignty a short time before, but when he heard of his father's death and of Odoacer's ferocity he went away, leaving the state without a leader.

Odoacer enjoyed such success with his plans that with the unanimous consent of his troops he constituted himself King of Italy; and for fourteen years, with no harassment from anyone, this Ruthenian ruled the Italians from the Citadel on the Capitoline Hill—the result of a clear gift from Fortune.

But now Fortune began to envy his tranquility and excessive splendor; and to decide his fate she, as it were, threw a fireball from farther than it is possible to imagine. Zeno, the Emperor, took a harsh view of Odoacer's occupation of Italy. He granted the Kingdom of Italy to Theodoric, the young King of Ostrogoths (and according to his best judgment a talented youth), if Theodoric proved able to conquer Odoacer with his army. Theodoric aroused his people to the prizes of war, and like a torrent they descended from Mysia through Firmum.[3] They entered Italy and for a short time refreshed themselves in a fertile spot by the Sontius River,[4] not far from Aquileia.

Odoacer was irritated that his peace had been disrupted. He gathered his troops together and moved out against the enemy, but was defeated in battle and

[2] Modern Pavia.
[3] From the Black Sea to modern Fermo.
[4] The Izonzo River.

fled to the interior. After he had reunited his forces at Verona, the Ostrogoth came there with his army, about to test Fortune once more in battle. Odoacer was easily defeated a second time. With the unhappy remains of his army he made a speedy march toward Rome, where he discovered that loyalty toward him had diminished because of these events. He and his army were denied entrance to the city, and in retaliation he devastated all the surrounding area with fire and sword and went to Ravenna. This city he strengthened against the enemy with new fortifications. But Theodoric by now had occupied all of Cisalpine Gaul and liberated it by defeating Gundobald, the King of the Burgundians. Theodoric left his supply train at Ticinum and came to Ravenna, where he besieged Odoacer for almost three years. He urged the citizens to surrender, giving them surety for their future safety. But when the unfortunate Odoacer was in the power of this harsh young ruler, Theodoric did not keep his pledge and, like the barbarian he was, executed Odoacer.

And so the man who in a sudden flight to the heights became a very glorious king believed that by an extended peace he could perpetuate himself in regal majesty. However, he was driven from his eminence step by step, until he sank to the depths of captivity. Joyous freedom never released the helpless man, and a hostile death bore him away.

ON THE PRESENT STATE OF THE CITY OF ROME

Rome still testifies to the civilization of our ancestors and the vacillation of Fortune.

Oh, most unhappy Rome! Into what darkness and sorrow have your avarice, dissensions, and mad ambition led you? To be sure, once you were the home of men who revered voluntary poverty, nor did they envy one another because of what they had except for the greatness of their virtues. You overcame the mountain heights, the seas, and the rivers; you were master of the northern snows, the Ethiopian sands, burning in the fervid sun. Neither dawn nor dark, nor the tiger of Hyrcania,[5] the elephant of India, nor the lion of Egypt could turn your legions. To your victories in arms, cities, peoples, and kings fell; and from every conquered province your leaders brought lustrous triumphs. By the efforts of your generals, you won the whole world as your spoils. You bowed the heads of all rulers, and your renown bore your most glorious name beyond the stars.

But now your condition is reversed. Most oppressed, you are so scorned as to have one of your consuls a Campanian, and you appease the wish of your rulers against some of your own citizens. You are reduced to this: your own princes are your principal enemies, the Africans, the deplorable Germans, who with all their might have always tried to efface your name. And what

[5] Proverbial for tigers. In reality the northern border of Iran near the Caspian Sea.

is worse, the Scythians, the Moors, and the Gauls arrived with their craving for booty, and safely turned their armies against you when your forces were exhausted and slothful, when you were emptied of all your citizens and forsaken by your rulers. Nor was this all, by any means, for you who once made the whole world your prize. Time and time again you were overrun by plunderers from every quarter and left stripped, deprived of everything human and divine. To the dishonor of the present rather than to the glory of the past, you witness both man's instability and, though it is half-decayed, the magnificence of antiquity.

ABOUT ARTHUR, KING OF THE BRITONS

After conquering almost all the world, Arthur is brought to defeat by the treachery of a bastard son.

While I was deploring the condition of our city, my eye fell on Boethius, and I must confess that the calamities of this very famous man moved me to write about him. I was drawn, first of all, by contemplation of his outstanding and venerable ancestors. Although the evil of the times had weakened and overthrown them, it could not dim the lustre nor destroy the name of the Manlius family, of which he was a member. Then there was the unique excellence of his studies, through which his reputation among philosophers shone more brilliantly every year.

But Arthur the King, in misery, came forward and stood in front of me. He has been famed in the celebrated English fables. Although we do not recognize the evidence of his greatness and his fate as worthy of credence, still let us surely relate his story, for subsequently the whole world seems to have given witness to him.

The Britons are situated in a western corner, almost separated from the rest of the world. According to their annals Arthur, at one time their ruler and the most famous king in the west, was descended from Constantine, who obtained the throne upon the death of Gratian, a native tyrant. Arthur's father was Uther, surnamed Pendragon, also one of the kings, and on his death Arthur, still young (though well brought up), ascended the throne. He realized that the power of the Romans was gone from the country, and that any man could take and keep what we wished of it without reprisal.

Arthur was not content with the power left him by his father, and increased it by the conquest of Ireland, the Orkneys, Dacia, Norway, the land of the Goths, and many other provinces. He then felt that his kingdom was large enough and his reputation ample, and decided to bring the wars to a close. Lest the warriors' virtue melt away because of inactivity, it is said that Merlin the Prophet, a man renowned in those days, ordered a table, which has been called the Round Table. As if to celebrate a feast-day, Arthur called to the table those knights that he considered the most noble, and with them formed a fellowship based upon laws and ordinances. The first and basic law was never to lay down their arms; then, to seek after wonders; when called upon, to defend the rights of the weak with all their strength; to injure no one; not to attack one another; to fight for the safety of their friends; to give their lives for their country; to seek nothing before honor; never to break faith for any reason; to practice religion most diligently; to grant hospitality to anyone, each according to his ability; whether in honor or disgrace, to make a report with the greatest fidelity to truth to those who keep the annals.

Many other praiseworthy laws were included, and all of them strictly observed. This fellowship, together with the power of his military alliances and the luster of his deeds, gave such brilliance to King Arthur's name that neither the ravages of Fortune nor the history of the ancients were able to affect it; it has come down to us in all its brightness.

Arthur, now happy, refused the Romans their customary tribute, and with the banners of his army flying, invaded Gaul, fighting against the consul, Lucius. Arthur was victorious and, his earlier desires for conquest reawakened, enlarged his attack. But now his pride paved the way for his death. While he pillaged the interior of Gaul, he left Modret, his son by a concubine, to defend the seat of the kingdom during his absence. The youthful Modret was strong and bold in all his actions, and for a long time had been spurred by a desire for power. He considered the absence of the king a chance offered to him by Fortune, and began to incite the oppressed to liberty, to capture the minds of all men with gifts, to guard the cities and the castles, and to show that he was going to be a very benign king. He called his friends together, trained men, and united a very large band of mercenaries. Then he denied victuals and help to his father, and did everything that had the appearance of a rebellion.

When the time was ripe, he published false letters stating that King Arthur had died in battle and that he, Modret, was to be king. Swift Rumor carried the news of these events into King Arthur's camp. The seat of battle was then suddenly changed, and the arms that

Arthur had led against the allies of Rome, he was now compelled to turn against his son. After gathering his troops together in a fleet, he sailed to the shores of England to crush the rebellion there, but he was not able to accomplish this. Modret left the shore and fled taking Guittonia with him. When he had reassembled his strength he decided to tempt the fortunes of battle.

Modret however, was of such obstinate faithlessness that he was not ashamed to fight against his father. When the battle began, the strength of Arthur's military discipline and of his soldiers' arms was marked, rendering the rebels conscious of the crime of attacking established power. For this reason they preferred death to defeat and could neither be driven forward nor turned aside. The battle was fought under a doubtful Mars, first favoring this side and then the other. On both sides there was a horrible slaughter, and almost all of Arthur's outstanding soldiers perished in this battle.

Arthur, grieving, pushed forward and saw Modret strutting about as if refreshed in strength and almost singlehandedly achieving victory, for he had put aside any affection for his father. Arthur took up a lance and a fresh mount, and with all the speed of the horse charged right at Modret, piercing him completely through his miserable body. But not without peril, for the youth, spurred by the deadly pain, gathered all his strength and struck a blow with his sword on the head of the approaching King. The helmet could not resist the blow, and the sword went all the way to the brain. The King, actually carried off by the horse, drew his lance from the dying Modret, and it is said that the wound was so wide that through it could be seen the rays of the setting sun. Modret, sinking on that spot, ended his evil presumption as well as his life. The King, however, knowing that this was his last day, came down from the horse and going to a boat, ordered that he be carried to the island of Avalon, and there death released him from his misery. He left the rule of the kingdom, its desolation, as well as the pursuit of vengeance, to his nephew Constantine.

Whether the death of Arthur was really kept a secret by his successor, or escaped notice in the tremendous confusion of affairs, is not known. But the fact remains that no one prepared a sepulcher for him, and many Britons think that he is not dead but held in a secret place, and continue to revere him as their eminent and distinguished king. They think that when his wounds are healed he will undoubtedly return.

What can be concluded from this? In a very short time Arthur's huge kingdom was shrunk and his own life lost through the temerity of one evil man. The famous Round Table, enriched by such brave men, was entirely deserted and broken up by Arthur's death, though it lives on in the fabulous tales of ordinary people. The triumphant glory of King Arthur and his brilliant renown gave way to shame and obscurity by this rebellion and destruction. From this example people can learn, if they wish, that in this world only the humble things endure.

ABOUT BRUNHILDIS,
QUEEN OF THE FRANKS

*The author and the Queen argue repeatedly over
the truth of her story.*

While I had not forgotten the shame which my famous
teacher had instilled in me because I was following my
own inclinations, I still was not entirely free from
idleness. I hoped to get started, if only I had a subject.
I was going over ideas in my mind when from afar
I saw Mahomet, the wicked deceiver. God knows that
with the greatest dilligence I listened to his deceptions:
how he eventually took the name of prophet, and, after
he had made some deadly laws, perished in his own
licentiousness. But a woman, more a she-devil, came
and dragged me away from him. Her hair was completely disarrayed; weeping copiously, she stood in my
way and said:

"Why do you neglect me, you who are tearing the
heart out of past calamities? Laboriously you have
hunted out others, but will not take what I offer. You
are silent, all the same I see you. You do not think much
of me, and you think that I'm only a servant girl. But
this hair that you see so neglected and bedraggled once
bore a queenly crown. Why do you turn your face
away, as if you were occupied with more pressing cares?
If you do not recognize me—I am Brunhildis, Queen
of the Franks. Why are you so unenthusiastic? Why do
you wish to turn to someone else? If you could treat
Cleopatra, the Egyptian, with some respect, why not
me?"

I was astounded to be addressed so unexpectedly and severely by this woman. Because I could think of nothing else to answer her very effective speech, I said:

"Brunhildis, although I have recorded the downfalls to the present time, there are more than I want. I feel sorry for your unhappiness, but I cannot grant your wish, for even now I do not remember ever hearing your name, nor about your fortunes."

She replied:

"You will never find anyone either more sweet or more bitter. I will tell you the story myself. Pick up your pen!"

I said to her:

"May I ask how I will be able to believe what you tell me about yourself? I have known since I was a boy that women have double tongues."

"Oh, woe is me!" she exclaimed. "Do you think that a queen lies?"

"If a crown changed the nature of your sex," I said, "I would not say so."

She responded:

"This is an old kind of misfortune that makes faith in what we say most difficult. I will tell you the truth, if I think it is appropriate."

"Can a few words from my pen console your deep grief? By Heaven, you should rather wish it erased from the memory of mankind than ask me to reawaken these half-forgotten stories by telling them all over again."

But she continued to insist.

"I want you to write what happened to me, what disgrace, what horrible cruelty I suffered as the mother of the King!"

I wished to work on something else, but as I was not made of iron, I changed my mind, asking:

"I will offer you the service of my pen if you will abide by this law: speak only the truth. Then, although I am busy, I will lend you my ears."

She poured out her tears abundantly, beat her breasts with such repeated blows that livid spots appeared; finally, still agitated with constant sobs, she replied:

"I think you have heard how Clovis, the ancient King of the Franks, had a son, Clothar, and from him a grandson. This grandchild, in turn, had four sons, and after his death, so that each of them could rule, the kingdom was divided into four parts. A war that had been prophecied broke out between Athanahild, my father and a descendant of Athalaric, the greatest King of the Goths, and other kings. Because of this, there was a great deal of suffering, but afterward there was peace. They made chains, as it were, to preserve it, and for this reason, while I was just a girl, I was given to King Sigebert in marriage."

I said:

"Be careful of what you say. I heard you were married to Chilperic or Childepert."

"I know that some people think this," she replied, "but as the end will show, I was married to Sigebert, to my hellish torment and rage. But what then? In the ripeness of youth, my beauty was at its height. There was not enough gold and jewelry enough to satisfy me. Raised to the royal throne, I saw myself admired and venerated by everyone as if I were a goddess come from the heavens. I was exalted by praises and honored above other illustrious kings. I gave birth to Clothar III, but oh, how I wish I had not, or that I had thrown him into a tomb at birth! While I was growing older and was enjoying all these joyous and very ample luxuries, a quarrel arose between the brothers, which immediately broke out in a war."

I said:

"Stop here! What was the cause of this quarrel?"

"Envy, as a result of the inequality of the kingdoms," she replied.

"A queen *does* lie," I said. "It was you, yourself, who sowed this melancholy seed in their hearts, for you always had an evil nature."

"A little while ago," she said, "this man did not know my name, and now suddenly he is a judge of my nature. Believe what you wish; it happened! After their minds were inflamed with hate, Chilperic, my husband's brother, was summoned under the pretense of arranging peace and was killed by a band of followers. And a little later, by the same misfortune, my husband was killed—for vengeance, I think." I would not stand for that:

"He was killed because of your treachery," I told her. "With the innate vanity of women, you were delighted with those who noticed your beauty. Too lascivious, and ignoring the condemnation of others, you ardently loved Landric, Mayor of the Palace. Defying the limits of feminine honor and, in spite of his own wishes and pleadings, you rushed to become his mistress. In this affair you used too little caution, and your sin was widely known, so you would not be punished (though you deserved it) you laid a trap for your unwary husband, who deserved better than that. In the middle of a wood, while he was returning from the hunt, you had him killed with a hunting spear."

Brunhildis was really upset because of this revelation and said:

"Who is this ignorant man that has become such a sharp disputant so quickly? Of course, I think that a person after these many centuries knows better what took place than I who was there! You are completely wrong. Fredegund was the woman who opposed Chilperic, his very beautiful wife. In telling you about the death of her husband I am more moderate than you are against me, for I did not give you her name. But let me finish. I was abandoned with a small child, and I had lost much of my past renown. But I took care of my court with what diligence I could."

I was impatient with her and said:

"Brunhildis, I have heard that Sigebert was not your and Clothar's son, as you say, but rather the son of Childepert. There were twins who survived his death, your grandchildren, Theodebert and Theoderic."

"You may believe what you wish," she replied. "For myself, I have started this story and I will not omit any part of it. It happens that Theoderic, my husband's nephew who ruled Burgundy, was angry with his brother Theodebert, King of Austrasia,[1] as well as with his wife and sons, because, as was reported, they were traitors. So he killed them."

I responded:

"I will not accept this any more than I did what you said before. This treason was your doing. I don't know where you get such skill of persuasion. But what shall I say? The desire for power does wonderful things. I think you were too eager for this. You had a great opportunity to sin without being punished, and in addition, there is a great natural tendency in women for evil. While you were often free of this tendency, still you did not learn to hold it back."

She replied:

"Without exercising your credulousness, I beg you, see how I escaped these ruses. After some time Theoderic, regretting what he did, tried to blame his evil

[1] Western Germany and eastern France, the land of the Merovingian Franks.

on others. He was killed by poison and his children by the sword."

Then I said this:

"I am not really being argumentative. This is truly how the deaths took place. I will tell about them, but I will supply what you have left out. Your crime stood in your way, and you removed it by poison and the sword."

She then became more tearful and said:

"I am unhappy because this man here thinks I am a liar. This is the way Fortune acts. She takes away faith in the words of those to whom she has given other good things."

I replied:

"I know whereof I speak."

Then for some time she chided me and denied what I had said. She said a good many things that were not true according to the evidence of many others. If I remained silent, she would think I believed what she said. She continued with her story, which I had interrupted so often.

"All these crimes and horrors committed against these illustrious nobles cried out for some sort of revenge. Clothar, now nearly grown up, went after it and wished to discover the perpetrator of such crimes. So far so good. Even left a widow by the king, I had the power to arouse the envy of many. Then some, driven by their hate, fed on my ruin and joined against me. I was accused by my son, was seized, and dragged into the palace. Here, in the presence of rulers and the strongest men, I, a woman and alone, was deprived of all help. I tried to tell my own story, not in the presence of judges, who should serve right on just and equal scales, but in the presence of my accusers. I was not only a woman and alone, but a Spanish woman among so many Franks, a widow, abandoned by her son, and a captive; could I get justice from enemies? What more can I say? I was conquered by my accusers with false testimony, false surmises, and many unspeakable tortures.

"My son, a boy, was easily led into this greatest of evils. By his order, I was handed over to the rulers of the kingdom, really my enemies, who, according to the nature of the crime against my innocence, passed sentence. Oh, how miserable I was! My son was not moved, neither by the breast from which he drew his first nourishment, not the wound which gave him birth, not the name of mother, even among the savage barbarians still venerated, not my tears. Although he was still a boy, he was as unmoved by my voice imploring his mercy as if he had been the most tenacious man. The terrible judgment was spoken against me, and when I heard it I protested in vain. No longer a queen, but like an ordinary street woman, I was handed over into the dire hands of the executioners, in view of all these people where I had often walked in a queen's regalia, accompanied by my nobles. They had forgotten their former reverence for me, tore off my clothes with their hands and left me naked.

"Oh, how strange! What is the strength of Fortune? I was unable to keep the tears from my eyes, but I saw no pity or tears for me in anyone else's eyes. Many pointed me out with their gestures, their eyes wide; they waited for something worse to happen to me. For a short time I could avoid them, but I could not shut my ears. Over the rumbling of the executioners, I heard the people cursing me, and my misery increased. What more can I add? Naked, I suffered the most disgraceful death. I was tied to the tails of strong horses by a foot, a hand and my hair. The horses were spurred in different directions, and I was torn apart. My name was dishonored, and among so many unbearable torments, my soul left my torn body."

Thus she had spoken, and, yielding to her wish, I have written her story, writing, I confess, without using enough trustworthy evidence; and so, if it is revealed that I have related something that is not true, it should be laid to the great effectiveness of her speaking.

A HUGE CROWD OF LAMENTERS

Dante does not wish to have his story told but prefers the story of one who brought shame on Florence.

I was still thinking about what I had just written when a dolorous crowd, greater than usual, appeared. Oh, how many heroes, how many famous leaders, how many princes, overthrown or injured, did I see? How this convinced me of Fortune's enormous and unbelievable power, by which many times those who really loved virtue were undeservedly thrown to the ground and trampled under-foot, and those who were truly evil and cared for nothing except vice, were lifted up to the pinnacle of honor and glory. Among the others was Philip the Fair, King of France, complaining that he was killed by a wild boar in the dark of the forest and that his death was regarded in Flanders as disgraceful and damnable. His three sons were with him, and cursed their untimely end and the adultery of their wives. But why should I be interested in these, for they obviously were not all whom there were among the plaintive marchers? I saw coming that most famous of men, one worthy of the highest praise, the famous poet Dante Alighieri. As soon as I saw his revered countenance that showed his remarkable endurance, I arose on the spot, and, going to meet him, I said:

"Why, oh, distinguished glory of our city, why are you marching in their mournful numbers, you who were so highly regarded of old for your endurance? Do you not think that I should relate the story of your notable ancestors, your works, most worthy of being remembered, your banishment from your ungrateful city, your laborious flight, long exile, and ultimate death under alien skies? You know, great father, that my powers are too weak for such a burden."

To this he replied:

"Stop, my son, and do not squander your words so volubly in my praise. Show something of your thrifty nature. I know your skill, and know what I have earned. I actually have no ideas concerning whom you should consider; nor should I be described as if I had come here conquered by Fortune. But loathing the stupidity of our citizens, I have come here so that you will not pass over those who brought her everlasting shame. So look over my shoulder to the one following me, a personal plague, a blot on the name of Florence. If you owe me anything, I wish that you would tell about his deeds and his fate, so that it would be clear to those who come after, those whom your citizens expel and those they receive."

I was about to respond, but he had already vanished from my sight. However, I saw the person he had pointed out to me coming with slow steps. I knew Walter, once Duke of Athens, the ruinous tyrant of Florence. He came with his face averted, his eyes fixed on the ground, wearing a mournful expression, tortured in mind and devoid of strength. Oh, how changed he was from the one who had first dared by stealth to tread upon the free backs of Florentines! But his story will be treated more fully.

ABOUT WALTER, DUKE OF ATHENS

Even the most savage of tyrants cannot withstand the united opposition of free citizens.

Walter, Duke of Athens, whose story we are about to construct, came from a French line, if we examine his ancestors, by blood noble enough, but in conduct ignominious. The former title his family bore was that of the counts of Brienne, but by what right I do not know they acquired the title of the Duke of Athens. It happened that the city of Lucca was besieged by Pisa. A little earlier, the Florentines had both paid out and promised great quantities of gold, and the city came under their jurisdiction. For this reason the Florentines assembled friendly citizens to lift the siege. They suffered a disaster, but after a few months had passed, the strength of the defeated forces revived. The news of the ensuing battle spread far and wide, and many strong young men with a great desire for war gathered there.

Meanwhile Walter in Naples put all other affairs aside and pretended to take a short trip. But secretly he left Naples with a few persons and took himself to Florence. Immediately he went to the siege, but because he came from so long a distance, he accomplished nothing worthy of note; and when Lucca fell to the Pisani, Walter retired to Florence. The strength of the Florentines was now much weakened as a result of this defeat and its unbearable costs, and the Senate was assembled to form a plan for the security of the state. Power would be given to a man experienced in war and with ample license to check the attacks of the enemies and the rebellion of the citizens. After much debate, this power, limited by the law, was given to Walter, as if to a friend of proven faith.

For a long time it brought hope to certain citizens, whom our ancestors called "grandi," to have a man in the city accustomed to and desirous of power and one who would take over the administration of the war. They were inclined to put this plan in operation. Foolishly they preferred the tyranny of a foreigner, whom they did not know, to the yoke of the law of the city to which they were accustomed. Having little confidence in himself, Walter joined with those citizens bound to debts outside the city, of whom there were then a great many. To gain time they easily agreed, after advice, to a wicked undertaking. Without delay, when they thought they had enough strength, they conferred with Walter (who was obliged to uphold the liberty of Florence as much by old as by new agreements) about subjugating the city to his power. He put aside his honor and his loyalty, and, driven by a strong craving for power, lent his ears to this counsel. He thought he would not attempt with arms what slowly he could obtain with subterfuge. After he had proved his faith to the others who were ruling the republic, he said that he could not accomplish anything for the public good unless further authority were granted him. And afterward this was done.

To show that he had not asked in vain, he executed some of the citizens. The signory of Florence were astounded, and perceived too late where Walter's request would lead. Rinieri di Giotto, to whom the magistrates had committed the affairs of Florence and the salvation of her people, let Walter's followers enter the city by night to oppose those who were about to rise up against the tyranny. He filled all the houses of the grandi with them, and thus the citizens were not able to refuse what Walter sought. By what sagacity they could, they tried to restrain his iniquity. They made a covenant with him that his power in the city would last only one year, and he confirmed by oath on the true body of Christ that when the year had passed, he would leave them their liberty.

Then he called all the citizens into an assembly, and when they and all the signory had gathered in the square in front of the palace, suddenly almost the whole place was filled with armed horsemen and foot soldiers, who had been sent there to surround all the citizens. Then the nefarious Walter arrived accompanied by a group of the grandi, all armed underneath their clothes. Thus protected, he announced that the unarmed people would drown in their own blood if there were any disorder. As he ascended to a higher place of council, the signory were squeezed in by a number of the grandi, who could scarcely refrain from laying hands on them. When this disturbance had subsided and there was silence, an orator ascended the rostrum to explain the agreement; but as soon as the clause about the rule for one year was made known, the ordinary people, advised ahead of time, began to cry out that it should be made perpetual. And immediately, by the work of the traitor Rinieri, the doors of the palace were opened to the tyrant and to his armed men. He entered and took it over.

As if they had not put their own liberty under the yoke but someone else's, the grandi began to celebrate the triumph of the enslaved people with dances. And those who owed money to others reveled in the fact that their creditors were now very poor. The lowest class surged everywhere. Idiocy took over the capital for its own. The people devastated everything, and celebrated the day by singing and scoffing. On that day no door was closed to anyone, no entrance denied, every house was open to all, and these idlers thought they—not the tyrant—had acquired power. The unfortunate signory, used to holding the seats of highest authority, were deprived of their sovereignty and sent into the basement cells of the palace while the tyrant occupied all the rest.

Walter began to run things just as he wished. To enforce the laws as well as to terrify the citizens, he set the most truculent men over them. He honored flatterers and befriended panderers; whoever was versed in the skills of evil, these he summoned into his council. He demanded a heavy tribute from the citizens, confiscated property, and converted everything to his own use. He had neither mercy nor compassion for anyone. Then with flattery, gifts, threats, and violence, he seduced both virgins and women for his enjoyment. He debased innocent young men, and permitted himself unspeakable excesses. In short, he defiled both man and God.

Because of the degradations, the miserable citizens, who originally had been worried and fearful but without any way to express themselves, began to complain. Too late they recognized that they had been deprived of the liberty they had known, and wished to overthrow and kill the tyrant. They condemned what he was doing, and if they got rid of him, they expected to restore their former freedom.

Discord is the root of a city's evil, for it allows no one to have faith in his neighbor. Because of this, those who were lukewarm to the tyranny suffered its bonds for a while longer. Finally God had compassion on their undeserved plight and permitted their eyes to be opened, so they could see the unhappiness of their

base servitude. With His strength He made their flicker-
ing hearts firm. He resolved differences and inspired
their assault on the tyrant. The grandi, who had joined
against the freedom of the people, were the first to acknowledge their own wickedness and withdrew their
loyalty from him. The leaders of the conspiracy secretly
and through intermediaries finally got the confidence of
the people, and they swore to overthrow Walter.

But while the opportunity was being arranged, the
tyrant learned of it, either because another person
revealed it to him or because of his own perception,
and tried with great cruelty to prevent it. He very quickly
brought disaster on himself. Those in the know learned
that some persons had been imprisoned and tortured,
and, fearing that they could not provide for their safety
alone, they armed and came out publicly, crying for
the death of the tyrant.

Oh, Heavenly Father, how marvelous are Thy judgments! Suddenly from everywhere the armed citizenry
gathered at the palace into which the nobles, the mercenaries of the tyrant, and those whom he had appointed
to rule the crowd had fled through the rear. There they
were besieged. Walter actually acted like a woman, and
was deeply affected by the great and unexpected change
in his fortunes. He exhorted those who were not yet
organized and were milling around to fight against the
people, but he, himself, worthless and trembling, finally
yielded to tears. He heard the cries of the besiegers
that filled the air and knew that his followers would
perish from hunger and thirst, and that tunnellers would
ruin the palace. Distraught by all these misfortunes
coming down on him from everywhere, he offered
through envoys to restore liberty if safe conduct were
given to him and his followers. To assuage a little the
savagery of those who were besieging him, he ordered

given over to them a certain assassin, Guglielmo da Scesi, more cruel than an animal, whom he had called a protector of the citizens, and his son, even more truculent than the father. Because of what he had done, God allowed this man, whose cruelty had bereaved many a parent, to see his own son torn to pieces in his presence. Also, a certain Arrigo, the worst kind of Florentine, who had confiscated the fortunes of the citizens, was hung feet down from a rafter like a piece of butcher's meat, and afterwards was cut up into little pieces. Yet what took place to harm Walter actually turned to his advantage, for all this violence softened the spirit of the citizens, and after a few days Walter got what he asked for.

Less than eleven months had passed from the day on which he took away our freedom until, frightened, he went away by night and left the city in its original condition. As a result, the great power that augured so well for the future, this arrogant man destroyed. Because of what he had unjustly appropriated, fame left a just ignominy. But so that the innocent city should not remain unavenged on the tyrant's injury, it happened—by God's judgment, it seemed to me—that while in arms against Edward, King of England, in the same battle in which John, King of France, was captured,[2] he decided to act differently from what he did in the beds of women, and faint-hearted, turned his back and abandoned the king. On his left he met the Florentine auxiliaries who, by chance, were fighting as mercenaries for John. Reprimanded by them, he was forced to go back into the battle against the enemy. He was thrown from his horse, and, as was reported, now weakened in strength because of a wound, he was recognized by

[2] The Battle of Poitiers, September 19, 1356.

another Florentine auxiliary fighting for King Edward. This auxiliary cut his throat. And so the man who wallowed in the blood of the Florentines, lost his life at the hands of a Florentine. The murderous, crafty, and evil Walter was overthrown, put to flight, and killed on that day, a death that came more quickly than it should.

AN EXCUSE BY THE AUTHOR
FOR PHILIPPA OF CATANIA

Why a woman of ordinary birth is admitted into this company.

At the very end of this work, by leave of the kings and illustrious persons, I will write of a woman of ordinary birth, but one whom they should not disdain. For, although her parents were of obscure ancestry and her end was very dreadful, yet in the midst of her prosperity Fortune was so flattering that she led a life among kings and royal ladies. Philippa of Catania, her hair dishevelled, showing all the blows of Fortune on her wracked body, begged with a trembling voice to follow after kings at least as a lady-in-waiting, if she could have nothing else. As I declared that I wished to describe the famous, not just the nobility; then, without injury to anyone, I could receive this supplicant. However, I thought I had good reason to include her; for I wish to point out that all this work, by its parts, seems to be arranged in some form: it started in happiness and will end in misery. It seems that the work began with the most noble of men, so it should end with a common and degenerate woman.

Therefore the success of the unhappy Philippa will follow as well as the remainder of her life. Since the novelty of her story is known to a few, they will be interested not in the story itself but in the way it is told. I have thought it not unsuitable to entwine the explanation with the story, so that the excessive brevity that is elsewhere a part of the narration does not take away from the purpose of the telling. I described what I saw with my own eyes, and I know that I was not deceived. In what I have heard, I have related the more truthful, and so I will not come to be refuted, I have sought out those who were more truthful. Now we will leave the other mourners, and for her beginning, let us go a little higher.

ABOUT PHILIPPA OF CATANIA

The daughter of a fisherman became Queen in everything but name, though still she died in misery.

While I was still a boy and employed at the court of Robert, King of Jerusalem and Sicily, Marinus of Bulgaria (an old man with keen memory originally a slave, and from his youth skilled in the art of sailing) was there. With him was Calaber Constantine da Rocca, a man as old as he was worthy of respect. These recounted the antiquity and nobility of the courts. Among other things they told how Robert, then Duke of Calabria, on the order of his father, King Charles, led an expedition against Frederick of Sicily, who was occupying the island.[3] After a while he had set up camp at Trapani, and here his wife, Violanta, gave birth to a son. Because

[3] Frederick II of Hohenstaufen.

of the lack of women, it happened that Philippa, whose story we have started, was made nurse of the little child. She was attractive in manner and appearance, but had been the daughter of a poor fisherman; only a few days before she had been washing the clothes of the foreigners. And when she had obtained the good graces of the Duchess, she came back to Naples and remained among the other servants, though the young child had died.

These two men told me that at that time there was a certain Raymond of Campagno, an Ethiopian, whose appearance did not detract from his character. He had been purchased from pirates by Raymond of Campagno, the prefect of cooks for King Charles. Because of his remarkable abilities, he was baptized, provided with Raymond's Christian and family name, and given his freedom. To him almost all the duties of the kitchen were assigned. Not long after, Raymond (the patron) went away to war, and the freedman was chosen to take his place. After that he had servants, horses, a house, and all the necessities. He began to attract the favor of the King and the nobles and to amass wealth. He was promoted from the kitchen to be Guard of the King's Wardrobe.

Meanwhile the Duchess wished to reward Philippa for her long service. Philippa was known as a widow, and since no one more suitable than Raymond was discovered, she was given to him as a wife. So that he might celebrate the marriage more joyfully and brilliantly, this audacious man asked that he be given a royal military command. When this was granted, the African soldier joined the marriage bed of this Sicilian washerwoman. According to the story of these old men, this was the beginning of her renown and nobility (or let me say more correctly, I have heard that this was Philippa's start).

Now we have nearly come to the things that I myself saw. Raymond, then, out of the service of the kitchen, had been made a soldier and enjoyed a famous marriage to Philippa, the Catanese. Among the soldiers Raymond conducted himself not inferior to any. He accomplished his missions and managed many commands. Above all he strengthened his own personal affairs with the greatest diligence. By this time Violanta had died, and Philippa, coming to Naples, with the greatest care submitted herself to Sancia, wife of King Robert, and to Maria, the wife of Charles, son of King Robert. She helped them, served them, and showed herself ever ready for their commands. She prepared and took care of their ornaments and various lotions and demonstrated that she was a perfect mistress. Thus affairs went. She exceeded in age the other women in the court, and was now the mother of three manly sons by Raymond, the soldier, and it seemed by long habit she had learned the customs of the court. She was appointed by the mother to be mistress and guardian to Joanna, daughter of Charles, Duke of Calabria. At this time Raymond was made Master of the Royal Household, and a short time after Charles and Maria died, and Philippa was honored as Joanna's mother. Raymond was made Royal Seneschal. What a ridiculous thing to see an African from a slave prison, from the vapor of the kitchen, standing before Robert, the King, performing royal service for the young nobleman, governing the court and making laws for those in power!

What does this mean, then? Just this. Fortune raises up whom she wishes. Thus a husband and wife are raised up; two of their children were married illustriously

and decorated with military honors. Also they had acquired towns, estates, villas, horses, numerous servants,
rich clothes, and all goods in abundance. You would
think they were the children of a king rather than of a
slave. Finally when Raymond died, he was buried with
almost regal rites, and his sons, who were soldiers,
began to carry on his duties. Then after several years,
when the youngest died, Robert, the third son, threw
off his clerical habit for that of a soldier. After some
more years the days ceased for the eldest son; Sancia,
the daughter, was left, just grown up, whom, from the
time she was a child, a grandmother had brought up
with Joanna as all of the same family. Robert, alone,
assumed the duties of his father and brothers.

When her husband and her sons were taken away,
Philippa's happiness was shaken, but with the passing
years her splendor glowed with greater brilliance. For
Joanna was given in marriage to Andrew, son of Charles
Humbert, King of Hungary, and when King Robert died,
Sancia, the Queen, went into a convent. Disputes arose
between Joanna and Andrew by the wicked urging of
certain persons. Andrew was despised, for the nobles
of the kingdom had sworn oaths to Joanna when Robert
was alive. By Joanna, Robert, from being the Seneschal
of the Court, was made Great Seneschal of the Kingdom,
and Sancia, his niece, was married to Charles, Count
of Marcone.

These extraordinary successes came to these Africans,
however, not without some spots on their honor. Though
it may not be right to believe it, it was said that the
pandering of Philippa was responsible for putting Joanna
into Robert's embraces. This crime requires a lot of faith,
for nothing serious, arduous, or great was accomplished
unless it was approved by Robert, Philippa, and Sancia.

No others except these must have known Joanna's secret.

But what then? We must leave these and throw suspicions to the winds. When there is the least familiarity
of any sort with a man, disgrace easily stains the most
honorable woman. But we must return to our story.
Philippa had now been raised to these titles and prefer-
ment, and it seemed to all that she had achieved everything except the name of queen. For Fortune was no
respecter of years. This exalted woman, now decrepit,
could expect only a little more time. In an unexpected
change of affairs she was covered with such calamity
that all her former splendor and honor seemed to turn
to her shame. Louis, King of Hungary, scarcely endured
that his brother Andrew be treated with such indignity
by Joanna and her associates because the former intention and last wish of King Robert was that Andrew be
given the crown of Sicily and Jerusalem by Pope
Clement. And now those who bore the order came to
Gaeta.

But some of the nobles of the kingdom, already knowing the severity of the royal youth, feared that perhaps
his anger was deserved, and if he were made king, they
saw they might be punished. Conspiring secretly against
him, they laid plans to prevent his being crowned. Who
they were and how they progressed against the boy is
not our present business. We have enough that pertains
to our purpose. By the stealth of the conspirators one
night in the city of Aversa, the boy was called from the
royal bedroom and ended his life in a noose. In the early
morning this accursed crime was discovered, and swift
Fame spread anger and outcry against the murderers in
all the city and the realm. In the first fury of revenge
certain young Calabresi, once chamberlains of Andrew,
were killed cruelly and dishonorably. Not satisfied with

these innocent lives, Hugo, Count of Avellino, by the consent of all the nobles, was commissioned to investigate what was known of the crime and to bring to judgment whoever was discovered. For what reason I do not know, he put into jail Robert of Campagno, Count of Trivulti, (until that time Grand Seneschal of Sicily) Sancia, Countess of Marcone, and the elderly and unhappy Philippa of Catania, as well as certain others.

Nor was there any delay. An immense oak barge was built in view of the city of Naples in the midst of the gulf, and while the people were observing, he tortured the unfortunate Philippa, Robert, and Sancia. What he drew from them is not known. However, it is held as reliable that they were guilty of the death of Andrew. After some days Philippa, Robert, and Sancia, nude, were bound to three poles, and in wagons were led through the city. The people gathered from everywhere and cried out against their shame. They were tortured with fire and pincers, and what was left of their miserable life ended in the flames.

This, therefore, was the end of Philippa. Indeed it would have been better to maintain her poverty by labor in the sea than to seek a better existence in luxury by criminal means. When condemned to the fire she lost her life and all that she acquired.

A LAST FEW MOURNERS AND
THE END OF THE BOOK

*The author's final advice on how to be a good ruler and
achieve happiness.*

Many readers think as I do that I will never bring my
pen to rest nor come to the end of my book. Many
princes arrived after the calamitous death of Philippa,
and the new ones wanted me to join their stories with
those others, if I were willing. Among them was Sancio,
King of Majorca, who complained that he had been
deprived of his kingdom by his maternal cousin, the
brother of the King of Aragon. After a disastrous battle,
his power had been smashed and he was taken prisoner;
by the order of the King of Aragon his head was cut off.

Then John, King of France, condemned his great misfortune. His kingdom had been lain waste far and wide
by fire and slaughter; it had been drained by plunder
and diminished by the occupation of the English, without valor and fearful, the most cowardly of men.[4] After
an ill-fated battle, John's forces had been disorganized,
broken, and put to flight, and many of his nobles had
been killed; he, himself, had been made a captive of
King Edward, and was deported to England.

John was followed by innumerable others, all complaining of their afflictions, but I decided to let them go,
for the time had come for rest. By God's goodness, we
have come through dangers, tears, and the ultimate fates

[4] An opinion generally held on the Continent in the fourteenth
century, because of the English use of massed longbowmen in
warfare, a weapon regarded as unknightly.

of many kings in our little bark. Sailing through the wide sea, we have arrived at the port toward which we first directed our prow. If, however, here and there, we have crossed either more or less of the sea than we should, and have deviated from the path of truth, I leave it to the correction of the wise. If, on the other hand, by this my labor, I have led anyone to the recognition of what he really is, and to humility, then I wish that any praise should be given to the bountiful grace of God.

You rulers, who have very great power in your hands, open your eyes and ears so that the sleep of death does not catch you by surprise. See how many of Fortune's spears, what different kinds, your body bears. And with your power do not refuse human counsels. No matter how strong something may be, it can be broken; no matter how piercingly bright, it can be obscured by a cloud. From the fates of others realize how perilous your state is. Avoid avarice, lust, wrath, boasting, and ambition, and be moderate in your pleasures. When your mind is filled with joy and something disturbs you, remember that you have risen by the same law as others, and that you too will fall into insignificance and be punished for your offenses, if it so pleases Fortune. And so you are not deceived by any kind of belief in the stability of satisfaction, fix this in your mind: Whenever anyone's situation seems to be taken for granted by ever-turning Fortune, then in the midst of this unfortunate credulity, she is preparing a trap. Far as we seem to be carried up to the stars, in the same way our hopes are very carefully planted in the depths.

So that you may have something to rejoice about in success, and something to alleviate your sadness in adversity, remember to give God the greatest veneration, and honor Him with all your emotions. Follow after wisdom and embrace the virtues. Honor those who are

worthy of honor, and serve your friends with great loyalty. Take advice from those who have shown wisdom,
and show kindness to those who are beneath you. Let
yourself overflow with mercy and justice. Search for
honors, praise, glory, and reputation, and show yourself
worthy of the majesty you have acquired. And if it happens that you are overthrown, then know it occurred
not because of your gift, but rather by the iniquity of
changing Fortune.